THE DEFENCE OF LUCKNOW

The large estate of Sikandarbagh was a scene of intense fighting in Lucknow in 1857. Contemporary accounts claim that more than 2,000 Indians were killed by British troops. The bones strewn across the foreground are supposedly the remains of these victims. The photograph was taken by Felice Beato and is featured here courtesy of the Anne S. K. Brown Military Collection, Brown University Library

THE DEFENCE OF LUCKNOW

T. F. Wilson's Memoir of the Indian Mutiny, 1857

Introduction by Saul David

Greenhill Books, London
MBI Publishing, St Paul

Greenhill
Books

The Defence of Lucknow

T. F. Wilson's Memoir of the Indian Mutiny, 1857

This edition first published in 2007 by Greenhill Books,
Lionel Leventhal Limited, Park House, 1 Russell Gardens,
London NW11 9NN
www.greenhillbooks.com
and
MBI Publishing Co., Galtier Plaza, Suite 200, 380 Jackson Street, St Paul,
MN 55101-3885, USA

The right of Thomas Fourness Wilson to be identified as the author of this
work has been asserted by him in accordance with the
Copyright, Designs and Patents Act 1988.

All rights reserved. No part of this publication may be reproduced, stored in or
introduced into a retrieval system, or transmitted, in any form, or by any
means (electronic, mechanical, photocopying, recording or otherwise) without
the prior written permission of the publisher. Any person who does any
unauthorized act in relation to this publication may be liable to criminal
prosecution and civil claims for damages.

Copyright © T. F. Wilson, 1857
Introduction © Saul David, 2007

British Library Cataloguing-in Publication Data

Wilson, T. F.
The Defence of Lucknow : T.F. Wilson's memoir of the Indian Mutiny, 1857
1. Wilson, T. F. 2. Lucknow (India) – History – Siege, 1857 – Personal narratives
3. India – History – Sepoy Rebellion, 1857–1858
I. Title
954.2'0317

ISBN 978-1-85367-723-6

Library of Congress Cataloging-in Publication Data available

Publishing History

The Defence of Lucknow was first published in 1858 by Smith, Elder, and Co.
and reprinted in 2007 by Greenhill Books with a new Introduction
by Saul David. The original despatch of Brigadier Inglis was appended by Smith,
Elder, and Co. in their first printing and has been retained in this edition.

The publishers would like to thank Dr Andrew Cook and everyone
at the Asia, Pacific and Africa Collections in the British Library
for their help in publishing this edition.

For more information on our books, please visit
www.greenhillbooks.com, email sales@greenhillbooks.com,
or telephone us within the UK on 020 8458 6314.
You can also write to us at the above London address.

Designed and typeset by MATS Typesetters, Essex

Printed and bound in Great Britain by
Creative Print and Design (Wales), Ebbw Vale

CONTENTS

List of Illustrations		6
Maps		8
Introduction		13
The Defence of Lucknow		17

Appendixes

I	*Captain Radcliffe's Narrative*	133
II	*Account of the Explosion at the Seikh Square*	136
III	*Division Orders by Major-General Sir J. Outram, G.C.B.*	138
IV	*From Brigadier Inglis*	141
V	*From the Homeward Mail*	163

ILLUSTRATIONS

Frontispiece: Sikandarbagh, scene of intense
    fighting in 1857

Lucknow, the capital of Oude	27
Entrance to Lucknow	37
Lucknow from the balcony of the Residency	46
Seikh Cavalryman	56
Elephants carrying troops to the camp before Lucknow	65
The head of the relieving force arriving at the Ballie Gate	75
Highlanders at Lucknow	85
Street in Lucknow	96
The King's Palace	105
The principal street of Lucknow	115

MAPS

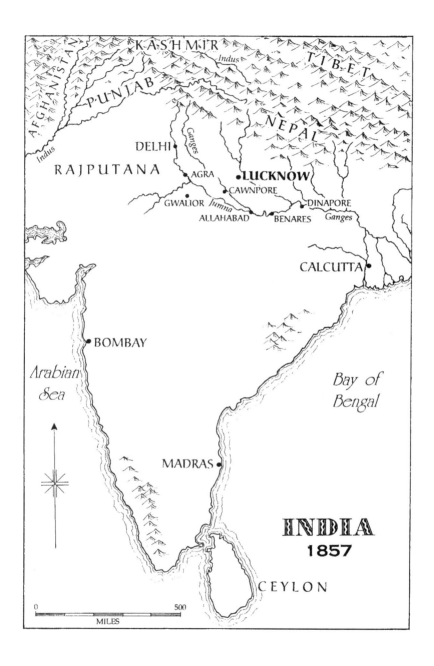

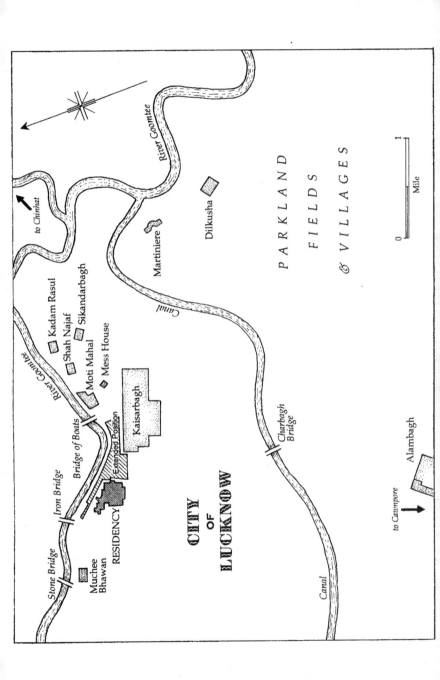

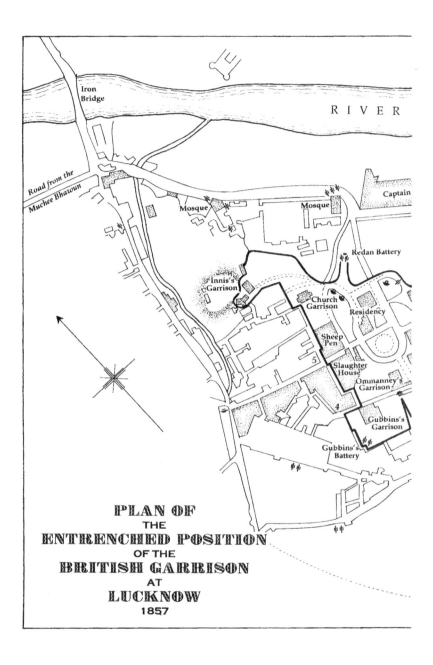

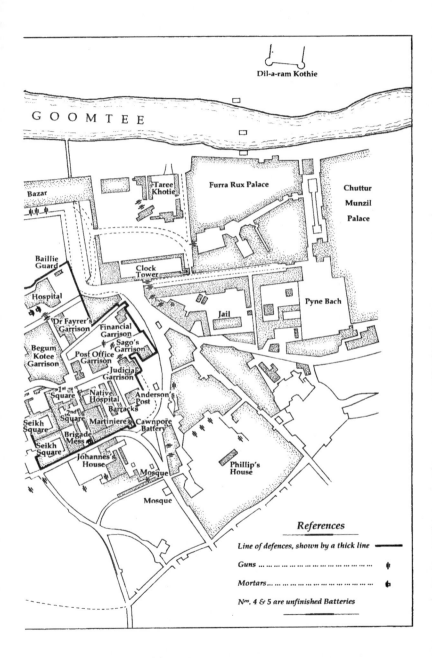

INTRODUCTION

First published anonymously in 1858, as the great rebellion against British rule in India still raged, *The Defence of Lucknow* is an eyewitness account of the first four months of the rising in the capital city of Oudh province, one of the epicentres of resistance. Its author, Thomas Wilson, was then a captain on the staff of the chief commissioner, Sir Henry Lawrence, and ideally placed to tell the inside story of this first phase of the epic siege of Lucknow's Residency.

The action begins on 30 May 1857 when, in imitation of earlier outbreaks across northern India, the native regiments in Lucknow rise against their British officers. Though forewarned by a loyal sepoy, Lawrence takes no pre-emptive action and a number of officers lose their lives as a consequence. Fortunately for the rest of the British garrison, the mutinous sepoys march away, giving Lawrence the opportunity to put the 30 acres of his Residency compound into an all-round state of defence. Less successful is the chief commissioner's hamfisted attempt to surprise the advancing rebel army at Chinhut on 30 June.

But it is Wilson's meticulous day-by-day record of the siege of the Residency – from the first rebel attack on 1 July to the long-awaited relief by General Havelock in late September – that forms the core of this wonderful diary. We learn of Lawrence's untimely death on 4 July (mortally wounded by a shell fragment two days earlier), the suffering of women and children ('crowded together in low, small, badly ventilated buildings'), the mounting casualties and the fortitude of the defenders, particularly the several hundred loyal sepoys, without whom the garrison would surely have perished.

We hear, too, of the desperate plight of the nearby Cawnpore garrison which, unlike Lucknow, had no British regiment to defend it. Finally, on 28 June, comes the news that everyone dreads: 'The Cawnpore force . . . had entered into a treaty with their enemies, after which they had all been treacherously murdered.' Determined not to share their fate, the Lucknow defenders fought on, though their clothes were tattered and their supplies dwindling fast.

Relief came at last as night fell on 25 September: 'The garrison's long pent-up feelings of anxiety and suspense burst forth in a succession of deafening cheers,' writes Wilson. 'From every pit, trench and battery – from behind the sandbags piled on shattered houses – from every post still held by a few gallant spirits, rose cheer on cheer – even from the hospital! It was a moment never to be forgotten.' Nor will it be while Wilson's remarkable account remains in print. Among the finest war diaries ever written, *The Defence of Lucknow* encapsulates the full cross-section of British experience during the Indian Mutiny: the shock of the initial risings, the horror of a lengthy siege and, finally, the exultation of rescue when all seemed lost.

Saul David
2007

THE DEFENCE OF LUCKNOW

MAY 20–30th 1857

FOR about ten days previous to the outbreak, daily reports were made that an *émeute* was intended, and Sir H. M. Lawrence had ordered all kinds of stores to be purchased and stored in the 'Muchee Bhawun' and the City Residency. But latterly the intelligence began to excite less attention, as so many days had passed away which had been named for the outbreak. On the evening of the 30th May, however, a sepoy of the 13th Native Infantry, who had shortly before received a reward from Sir Henry Lawrence for having assisted in the capture of a spy, came to Captain Wilson of the 13th Native Infantry, Assistant Adjutant-General, and said he could not help reporting that there would be a rising amongst the sepoy regiments, to be commenced in the lines of the 71st Native Infantry that evening at about 8 or 9 p.m.; but he was not certain at what hour. His manner in giving this information was *earnest* and *impressive*.

On that evening everything went on as usual; all remained quiet in the cantonments, where Sir Henry Lawrence was residing. Some days previously the ladies and children had been removed to the Residency in the city, which place had already been occupied by a party of the 32nd Foot and two guns. The 9 p.m. gun was fired, and was evidently the preconcerted signal for the mutiny; for a few minutes after, whilst Sir Henry Lawrence and his staff were at dinner at the Residency, a sepoy came running in and reported a disturbance in the lines. Two shots were heard in the 71st lines. The horses of the staff were at once ordered, and they

18 THE DEFENCE OF LUCKNOW

proceeded to the lines. On the way, more dropping shots were heard from the left of the 71st lines. The party arrived in the camp, where about 300 men of Her Majesty's 32nd, with four guns of Major Haye's battery, and two guns of the Oude Irregular Force were posted, and found them all on the alert. These were posted in a position on the extreme right of the 71st lines (the whole front of which they swept), and they were also contiguous to the road leading from cantonments to the city.

Sir Henry Lawrence immediately took two guns and a company of the 32nd with him on the road leading to the town, and there took post; thereby blocking up the road, and effectually cutting off all access to the city. He sent back soon after for reinforcements of the Europeans and for two more guns. In the meantime, the officers of the several regiments had proceeded at once to their res-pective lines. Bands of insurgents had meanwhile made their way amongst the officers' bungalows, keeping up as they went a desultory fire, which prevented many from passing the roads towards the lines. One of the first of these parties made straight for the mess house of the 71st Native Infantry, whence the officers had escaped but a few minutes before. They exhibited great blood-thirstiness, making every search for the officers, and ending by firing the house. On several shots being fired from the 71st lines on the 32nd Foot and guns, the order was given to open with grape; on which a rush was made by the sepoys to the rear; when they passed the infantry picket, which is situated in the centre of cantonments. The picket was under the command of Lieutenant Grant of the 71st Native Infantry. His men remained with him till the mutineers were close upon him. They then broke; but the subadar of the guard, and some men of the 13th and 48th Regiments, composing the guard, tried to save

MAY 20–30th 1857

19

him by placing him under a bed. A man of the 71st Native Infantry, who was on guard with him, however, discovered the place of his concealment to the mutineers, and he was there brutally murdered – receiving no less than fifteen bayonet wounds, besides some from musket balls.

From the first, Lieutenant Hardinge, taking with him some few sowars of his Irregular Cavalry, patrolled up and down the main street of the cantonments, and went to the officers' messes on the chance of saving any lives. In the compound of the 71st mess, he was fired at by a mutineer, who then rushed upon him with his bayonet, which pierced his arm. More than once the cantonments were thus patrolled by Lieutenant Hardinge under a smart fire, with the same humane intentions; but not in sufficient force to prevent the burning and plundering of the officers' bungalows, and of the bazaars. The excitement in the lines continued; while the 32nd remained quietly in position, awaiting the advent of the remnants of the regiments who had remained true to their colours. A remnant of the 13th Native Infantry, about 200 men, with colours and treasure, came up; and, according to previous arrangement, joined and fell in on the right of the 32nd. A small portion of the 71st, without being able to save their colours or their treasure, (through the disaffection of the native officer on duty,) also came up and took post next the 32nd Foot. Of the 48th, nothing was heard till 10 a.m. next day. About 10 o'clock p.m. many of the mutineers had made their way up to some empty artillery lines, outside the 71st Native Infantry lines, whence they commenced firing. Brigadier Handscomb, who had come up from the rear of the 71st lines, was killed by a stray shot from this place: just as he had reached the left flank of the 32nd, he fell dead off his horse. The bungalows throughout the cantonments were most of them on fire. No attempt was subsequently made to attack the position. To secure the Residency bungalow, and that portion of the cantonment next the city road, 4 guns and a company and a half were taken up to the cantonment Residency, and the guns placed at each gate. All was now quiet, and the remainder of the night passed away without any further event. Nothing had been seen or heard of the 48th Native Infantry. Many officers had most wonderful escapes from death. Lieutenant and Adjutant Chambers of the 13th Native Infantry, was severely wounded in the leg, whilst effecting his escape from the magazine where he had taken a guard of his regiment.

May 31st – At daylight, the force, consisting of some companies of Her Majesty's 32nd Foot, and the remnants of the native regiments, about 100 men 71st, and 220 men 13th Native Infantry, with part of the 7th Cavalry, and four guns, advanced down the parade in front of the lines of the several regiments. From the lines of the 13th Native Infantry about fifty men came, and said they had saved the magazine of that regiment. Hearing that the body of the rebels had retired towards the race course, where they had plundered the lines of the 7th Cavalry, and murdered Cornet Raleigh of that regiment (who had been left there sick) the whole force of cavalry and infantry, with four guns, proceeded thither, leaving Colonel Case with a portion of the 32nd in position in cantonments. On arriving in the open plain, a body of about 1200 men were seen in line in the distance, drawn up to the race course. Many of the cavalry galloped over at once to the insurgents. The guns then opened with round shot, which dispersed them, and they made the best of their way across country, followed immediately by

MAY 31st 1857 21

the cavalry and guns, and, at a greater distance by the infantry. No opportunity offered for the guns to again open, owing to the celerity of their flight; but the cavalry hovered round and took about sixty prisoners, who were brought into cantonments. The pursuit continued in the same order until the guns were stopped by a nullah, over which they could not cross. The cavalry, however, continued their pursuit, and kept it up for some ten miles. By 10 a.m. the force had returned to cantonments, as the heat was excessive.

As most of the bungalows were burned (the officers having lost everything) the troops were moved into camp, – the 32nd and guns into the position they held formerly; the native regiments next them on the right, and in the following order:– 13th next the 32nd, the 71st next, then the 48th, with the 7th Cavalry on the extreme right. The usual guards were kept by the native regiments, and the cantonments regularly occupied. Owing to this, the neighbouring country seemed to be reassured. Supplies came in regularly, and in plenty. The exertions of all were redoubled to complete the defences, and collect stores and supplies in Muchee Bhawun and the city Residency. The former post, originally occupied by the dependants of the late king, had been selected by Sir Henry Lawrence as a fitting place of security and retreat, in case matters took an unfavourable turn. On the 16th of May, immediately on the receipt of intelligence from Meerut of the commencement of the outbreak, this stronghold, then in a very dilapidated condition, was occupied by the light company of the 13th and some guns, and measures were taken for its thorough cleansing. Supplies continued to be brought in and stored.

On the evening of the day on which the troops returned from the pursuit of the rebels, an insurrection took place in the city towards Hosainabad; the standard of the prophet was raised, and other means of religious persuasion used to excite the populace. The police of the city, under the energetic superintendence of Captain Carnegie, behaved well, and the movement was at once quelled, and the standard taken. News of the *émeute* at this place had by this time reached the district, and the rising of the neighbouring stations was to be looked for.

On the afternoon of the 4th June, parties of ladies and officers of the 41st Native Infantry, escorted by about twenty-five men of the regiment, who had remained faithful, came in, bringing the news of the mutiny at Seetapore, and of the deaths of Lieutenant-Colonel Birch, commanding the regiment there, of Mr. Christian, and of other civilians and ladies. On the 5th, news came of the mutiny at Cawnpore, but no particulars. Reports of all kinds were rife among the Bazaars; but no authentic intelligence could be procured, as the telegraph wire was cut. From Benares the news came in of the 37th Native Infantry having mutinied, and of their having been overpowered by the rest of the force there. But nothing further transpired, for from that day to the 10th instant, the communication was *in toto* interrupted.

June 10th – The defences at the city Residency, as well as the Muchee Bhawun, were increased, and houses and buildings around them began at once to be demolished. Large stacks of firewood were made, and houses and tents set apart for the occupation of the European refugees, who were arriving from the districts daily. Provisions of all sorts continued to be stored, including 110 hogsheads of beer just arrived from Cawnpore.

Besides the two important posts noted above, the range of buildings towards the Hosainabad quarter of the town were occupied by 2000 police under the direction of Captain Carnegie; a thousand more were ordered to be raised, and officers of the 41st were put in command of each of the police battalions. This day we heard, by native report, that General Wheeler was defending himself in the entrenchments at Cawnpore; but no letter was received.

June 11th – Early this morning a false alarm was brought in from the Cawnpore road, that the enemy was upon us. Captain Evans, who had been sent out to gain information, returned with the above report, which created for a short period some needless alarm. We continued hard at work getting in supplies and adding to our defences. Many vague reports of disturbances were in circulation to-day.

June 12th – On this day an instance of disaffection from within the camp occurred. The regiment of military police, commanded by Captain Orr, mutinied in a body, rushed to their lines, seized their arms, and then set off in the direction of Cawnpore, giving themselves no time to inflict any damage in their quarter of the city. So great was their haste, that they failed to empty their own barracks, and left behind them their clothes and baggage. Information of this was given to head quarters; on which two guns of Major Kaye's battery, two companies of Her Majesty's 32nd, and some seventy Seikhs of the 1st Oude Irregular Cavalry, the whole under the command of Colonel Inglis, were despatched after them. They were pursued for some eight miles before they were come up with, and it was only by pushing on the cavalry and guns, without waiting for the slower movements of the infantry, that they were overtaken at all.

24 THE DEFENCE OF LUCKNOW

The guns opened fire as soon as practicable; they had come up well over some difficult ground, but their horses were, in consequence; so done up, that there was some difficulty in taking up the most desirable position. Once the cavalry charged well, but neither the result of their charge, nor of the practice of the artillery, was such as might have been expected. The enemy's loss was not exactly ascertained, but it was supposed that they had some twenty killed, and ten prisoners were brought in. Of Captain Forbes's men, two Pathans were killed on the spot; and some others, including a gallant old native officer, wounded. Mr. Thornhill, of the civil service, charging with them, was also wounded. All this time the infantry were far behind, unable to get up. A village lay to the front, in which many of the insurgents had taken refuge. Colonel Inglis forbade its bombardment, as it would have entailed much injury to innocent villagers; and the evening was, by that time, so far advanced, that the measure would probably not have sufficed to dislodge the mutineers.

About an hour remained to sunset; the guns and cavalry were a long way from the infantry, and many miles further from home. A return movement was therefore ordered, and accomplished successfully: the whole force returned about 8 o'clock, having gone over some sixteen or eighteen miles of ground.

The Europeans had marched well to the front. It was a hard day's work for them, and two men were lost from apoplexy, for the heat was dreadful.

On this day the horses of the men of the 7th Cavalry were brought down and picketed close to the Baillie Guard; as, with a very few exceptions, the 13th, 48th, and 71st Regiments of Native Infantry and 7th Cavalry had been ordered to proceed on leave till October, and

JUNE 12–14th 1857   25

their arms and accoutrements were brought down and deposited in the Residency. (Vide No.1 in the Appendix.)

June 13th – Shot and shell both brought down to the garrison from Muchee Bhawun (about three-quarters of a mile). Unabated exertions to add to the defences of the garrison.

The 13th Regiment of Native Infantry, 170 rank and file, came down from cantonments and encamped in the Residency compound. Ineffectual efforts to blow down the *Furrahd Buksh* Gateway. Three or four cases of cholera occurred at Fort Muchee Bhawun. Officers' servants began to desert. Intelligence was received from Fyzabad of the mutiny of all the troops there. Heat beyond endurance. Garrison in good spirits, and much elated at the brush after the Police Corps. Little reliance was placed in natives, and every possible precaution was taken to prevent any treachery. The native gunners, both in the Residency and at the Muchee Bhawun, were so posted as to be under the immediate fire of the Europeans, who watched them carefully both day and night. An officer was on duty at the gate all day long, to observe all incomers, and to prevent arms being brought in by others than those who had received passes.

June 14th – Supplies of shot and shell brought in from Muchee Bhawun. Every exertion made to increase the defences of the garrisons. No reliable intelligence was procurable of the state of affairs at Cawnpore. Many idle rumours afloat, but not corroborated, with regard to a reinforcement of Europeans having arrived at that station from the north-west. Heat excessive. Several cases of cholera and smallpox. A few cases of the former disease proved fatal in Muchee Bhawun. Hardinge's

Corps still steady. About 200 of the Oude Irregular Cavalry deserted last night.

June 15th – A hundred barrels of gunpowder brought from the Muchee Bhawun, and buried in the Residency enclosure. Shot and shell continued to be brought into garrison from Muchee Bhawun. Uncovenanted servants were drilled with muskets. A tragic event occurred this day: – Serjeant-major K., 7th Light Cavalry, shot with a pistol, Riding-master Edridge, 7th Light Cavalry, in the heat of an argument. The riding-master died a few hours after. No reliable intelligence was procured from Cawnpore, though vague reports were in circulation. The death of Lieutenant Colonel Fisher, commanding 15th Irregular Cavalry, by the hands of his own men, was reported.

Captain Gall's servant returned to the garrison this day, reporting his master's death, which took place by stratagem, and by the hands of his own men. Captain Gall was proceeding in disguise *en route* to Allahabad, with twelve sowars of his own corps, and had proceeded about fifty miles on his way, when his murder took place. All officers of the cantonments were ordered down to the garrison, with the exception of the commanding officers and regimental staff. Twenty-three lacs of rupees were buried close in front of the Residency, for security, and to avoid the necessity of guards and sentries over it. Rum and porter (one-half) was received into the Residency from Muchee Bhawun. Fever was prevalent. The Seikhs of the 13th Native Infantry, numbering about fifty men, were formed, at their own request, into a company, under the command of Captain Germon, and sent to Muchee Bhawun. Spare clothing of the 13th was brought in from cantonments. Continued efforts were made to blow up

Lucknow, the capital of Oude

the Furrah Buksh Gate. The flooring of the first story fell in this day.

June 16th – A quantity of shot and shells came in from Muchee Bhawun; also an 18-pounder gun. The shot was piled, as far as possible. On this date, there were seven 18-pounders in position. The whole day was expended in working hard at a battery in a position commanding the Cawnpore-road, and in unroofing houses, burying powder, &c. The gate leading into the Furrah Buksh came down in the course of the forenoon with a great crash, after many futile attempts had been made for its destruction. This was an important point gained, as the Residency compound was quite commanded from the top of this gate.

This morning, twenty-two conspirators, emissaries from Benares and elsewhere, who had been sent to corrupt the troops at this place, were captured in a house in the centre of the city. Information having been given to Captain Hughes, commanding the 4th Irregular Infantry, he directed two staunch native officers to put themselves on the watch, and to pretend participation in the disaffection. This they did, and by this means, with Captain Carnegie's assistance, Captain Hughes was enabled to effect the capture of these inciters to mutiny. They were forthwith brought to a drum-head court-martial and the whole of them condemned to death.

June 17th – This morning, four of the men sentenced yesterday, were hanged at the Muchee Bhawun; the remaining eighteen were liberated, as some doubts were entertained of their guilt.

Vague and most contradictory rumours came in this day about Cawnpore, but no authentic intelligence could be gained. The intelligence department, under the supervision of Mr. Gubbins, with two assistants, seemed to experience great difficulty in procuring reliable intelligence. Amongst others, Colonel Palmer, commanding the 48th Regiment Native Infantry, came in from the cantonments, waited on the Brigadier-General, and reported large assemblies of men near cantonments, the immediate abandonment of which he most earnestly advocated.

Although there yet remained some twenty-five lacs in the treasury, the expenditure had been on such an enormous scale during the last week, that cash payments were suspended, unless in exceptional cases. The money rewards, &c., promised to men of the several infantry regiments, whose good behaviour had been conspicuous on the night of the mutiny, were discharged by promissory notes. Major Apthorp of the 41st Native Infantry had an advance made to him to pay up and discharge twenty-five of his men who had escorted in the officers and ladies from Seetapore; as it was reported by one of his drummers, that even these faithful few, who had all been promised promotion by Sir Henry Lawrence for their fidelity on that occasion, had expressed themselves to the effect that if Rajah Maun Singh came against them, they would all have to go over, and would murder their officers.

June 18th – The force at the Residency, consisting of the regular troops, civilians, volunteers of all sorts, and, in fact, every man within the defences not incapacitated by sickness, were ordered by Sir Henry Lawrence to parade at sunrise. Every man was to be at the post he was to occupy in case of an attack; and those to whom no posts had been assigned mustered in front of the Residency, for the purpose of having a post or duty assigned them. The Brigadier-General inspected the whole of them, and visited all the outposts and picquets.

In the evening of the same day the force was paraded a second time, and minutely inspected by Colonel Inglis. A body of fifty volunteers, belonging to the several offices, had been trained and drilled to use firearms. To them was entrusted the defence of two outposts near the Post-office, which place had been made a very strong position. The officers comprising the volunteer corps of cavalry were also given arms, to be able to make a stand and defend themselves within their own quarters. They furnished sentries at night, and exercised a supervision over some seventy Seikh sowars; the remains of the Oude Irregular Cavalry. These, as well as the body of clerks, &c., mentioned above, were in all respects armed and accoutred like private soldiers. Besides this, many of the

30   THE DEFENCE OF LUCKNOW

volunteers and officers were instructed in gun drill; and, at the Muchee Bhawun, by Sir Henry's directions, some fifty or sixty of the 32nd Foot were told off for the same work. A very strong battery (the Redan) was commenced this day; it completely commanded the iron bridge and the road leading to cantonments.

The servants of Captains Staples, 7th Cavalry, and Burmester, 48th Native Infantry, returned and reported the murder of those officers whose heads, they stated, were carried to the Nana at Cawnpore; and that Lieutenant Boulton, of the 7th Cavalry, jumped his horse into the river, and nothing further had been heard of him. Owing to the want of rain, the heat had now become intense. Cholera and dysentery were on the increase; chiefly at the Muchee Bhawun.

Reports came in of some bodies of the enemy being at a place called Nawab Gunge, about eighteen miles from Lucknow, and Captain Forbes, with twenty Sikhs and ten of the volunteer cavalry corps, was sent out there to ascertain the presence or otherwise of the enemy. They returned in the evening bringing information that there was no one. The company of the 10th Oude Irregular Force was brought down from the Dâk Bungalow to the jail. This regiment was the last to give way at Seetapore, and it was reported they did not molest their officers.

Quantities of bhoosa were collected and stored within the Racket Court, which was now half full.

June 19th – This morning Sir Henry Lawrence inspected the Muchee Bhawun minutely. More small arm ammunition was brought in from thence to the Residency.

A fresh case of small pox occurred to day (Mr. Bird, who was immediately removed to a tent in the compound). The uncovenanted volunteers were again minutely inspected this afternoon. The engineer officers were very hard at work completing the batteries and defences. Upwards of 3000 coolies were at work unroofing houses in the vicinity of our defences.

From cantonments all the spare baggage, &c. was brought in, and every preparation made to prevent confusion in case the position there should be abandoned. In the city of Lucknow everything remained perfectly quiet, – the administration of justice was in no way impeded. Grain was stored in large quantities in the church.

June 20th – This day, 'the Redan' was completed. It consisted of one 18-pounder gun and one 9-pounder, with two mortars in their rear – the whole commanding the iron bridge and open country across the river. The Cawnpore 18-pounder battery was very nearly finished, and an expense magazine establishment near it.

A letter bearing date the 18th instant was received from Cawnpore, written by Captain Moore of Her Majesty's 32nd Foot, by direction of General Wheeler, – it informed us, at last, of occurrences at that place. All the numerous previous reports regarding the reinforcements of European troops said to have been received, were thereby falsified. No such reinforcements had ever been received. The letter informed us of their ability to hold out for some fifteen days more. The dreadful news of a boat load of European ladies, women, and children, from Futteghurh, having been intercepted at Cawnpore and assassinated there, was confirmed by natives.

Supplies continued to be stored, but they were collected with difficulty and at increased prices.

Large stacks of firewood, which had been stored in case of difficulties, were regularly arranged in a semi-

32 THE DEFENCE OF LUCKNOW

circle, protecting the front of the Residency, and covered with earth; these formed an embankment six feet in height, and embrasures were cut through them for the guns, of which there were four 9-pounders on that side.

June 21st – Two hundred guns, many of large calibre, were found in the gardens of the Seish Mahul, behind the Dowlut Khana (a large building on the north side of the city). There were no carriages to them. This startling discovery was luckily made in time. Twenty-seven guns were at once brought in, and arrangements made for parking the remainder.

In the evening, as the church was full of grain, divine service was performed in Mr. Gubbins's garden; and, during the night, Sir Henry himself once more visited the outposts, which had, by this time, been brought to a satisfactory state. The guards of the uncovenanted service were well on the alert, and prepared for any emergency. The difficulty of procuring all kinds of grain daily increased. Many rumours of a strong force marching on Lucknow from Fyzabad. The force in cantonments held in readiness to march at one hour's notice, to the Residency and the Muchee Bhawun.

June 22nd – This morning Captain Radcliffe's troop of volunteer cavalry were despatched, at 1 a.m., towards Nawab Gunge, to patrol the roads in that direction, in conjunction with the Seikhs, in order to gather information. About 4 o'clock a.m. a thunderstorm from the east, with the much wished for rain, came on. It lasted no very long time, and afforded only a temporary relief from the excessive heat.

Sir Henry Lawrence made an excursion as far as the Husainabad Kolwallee, garrisoned by nearly 3000 police

JUNE 22–23rd 1857

and others, and inspected them and the defences of that place. He also visited the Dowlut Khana, an old magazine, and on his return went over the Muchee Bhawun defences. All our available spare carts, hackeries, and wagons, were to-day employed in bringing in the guns found yesterday. Many of them were of large size. The unroofing and clearing away of houses continued without intermission, and every exertion was made to remove anything which might afford cover in the immediate vicinity of our defences.

June 23rd – Two men executed this morning at the Muchee Bhawun, – the one a mutineer (a naick of the 71st Native Infantry), the other a man who had, on the night of the mutiny, threatened the life of Mr. Yarbury, a merchant.

A large battery traced out, looking to the westward. It was to consist of at least two heavy guns, and to be raised so as to bombard the town in that direction. A considerable amount of labour would have been required to raise it to the necessary elevation. Altogether it was the most extensive work of the kind we had yet undertaken. An 8-inch howitzer, which had been discovered with the other guns at the Seesh Muhal, was mounted and placed in the Redan battery.

Captain Radcliffe's troop of volunteers, numbering forty sabres, were drilled and exercised daily; and now that the majority of the Irregular Cavalry had deserted, and the remainder were not considered trustworthy, the troops supplied two mounted orderlies every morning to escort Sir Henry Lawrence into the city.

The commanding officer of the 71st Regiment Native Infantry reported the remnant of the Seikhs of his regiment (about twenty men, who had remained true on

34 THE DEFENCE OF LUCKNOW

the night of the *émeute*) as being in an insubordinate state, and no longer to be trusted. Sir Henry Lawrence desired them to be sent to him, and spoke to them. They had asked for their discharge before, and had very precipitately been disarmed by their commanding officer, without sufficient authority. After being spoken to by the Brigadier-General, they professed themselves quite willing to continue their services: they were taken at their word, their arms restored, and were kept at the Residency under the command of an officer.

A letter was received yesterday from Cawnpore, written under the direction of General Sir H. M. Wheeler, K.C.B., giving very bad news indeed. It stated that the enemy shelled them for the last eight days, which had had fearful effect within their crowded trenches, and one third of their number had been killed.

In the meantime, the Muchee Bhawun garrison had not been idle at their defences, and Sir Henry was constant in his visits there, as well as to the Seesh Muhal, and Dowlut Khana. On the westward side of the Muchee Bhawun, a heavy tower was commenced; a work of great labour, from which a flanking fire could be given. In the vicinity of the fort, as at the Residency, houses were unroofed, and walls pulled down, so as to leave as little shelter as we could. Magazines were constructed, and the powder placed in safety.

June 24th – Heavy clouds, and every appearance of rain throughout the day, but none fell. Heat excessive. Sir Henry Lawrence proceeded at daybreak as usual, attended by his staff and two orderlies from the volunteer cavalry, and inspected the Dowlut Khana, Seesh Muhal, Imaumbarah Kolwallee, and Muchee Bhawun; and in the evening he proceeded five miles on

JUNE 24–25th 1857

the Fyzabad road, to ascertain if there was a good position we could take up, in case of an advance of the rebels in that direction.

The last of the guns discovered in the Seesh Muhal garden were brought in to-day. Four of them were of very large calibre – two being 32-pounders. *Native* reports describe the force at Cawnpore as being hard pressed. Native reports from Allahabad were good. Much progress made in knocking down and unroofing the houses in the *immediate* vicinity of the Muchee Bhawun and Residency. The Racket Court was now filled with bhoosa for the cattle, and thatched in. We were supposed to have nearly three months' supply of provisions now stored. The mutineers were reported to have arrived at Nawabgunge (eighteen miles distant), and were said to have with them some sixteen guns.

June 25th – The tower at the Muchee Bhawun was carried on this day with great ardour. Crowds of coolies were employed under the direction of Lieutenant Innes of the Engineers. This defence was to command the stone bridge, the Imaumbarah, and a number of high mosques facing that side of the Muchee Bhawun. Elephants were yoked to one of the heaviest guns, – luckily there was some gear for the purpose, and the experiment turned out successful.

A native rumour reported the arrival of a strong force of mutineers at Nawabgunge, where it was said they were to remain till they had consolidated their force. Good news came in to-day from Allahabad in a letter from the officer commanding the 1st Madras Fusileers, dated the 18th of June, in answer to one despatched from this place on the 15th instant. Colonel Neil's letter gave little or no detail, beyond stating that he assumed

36 THE DEFENCE OF LUCKNOW

command of the fort on the 11th instant; that there had been much fighting, but all the mutineers were entirely broke and dispersed, and the cantonments reoccupied. Cholera broke out on the 18th among the Fusileers, who in two days had had amongst them 100 cases, forty of which had proved fatal. Every effort was being made to push on troops to Cawnpore, but the road was not open, and carriage was difficult to procure: also that Her Majesty's 84th were close at hand, and that the telegraphic communication had been re-established between Calcutta and Allahabad. No authentic intelligence from Cawnpore, and much anxiety was felt regarding the force there.

All appearance of rain had gone off, and the heat was almost insupportable. The river had risen about a foot and a half, and was no longer fordable. A letter was received from Mrs. Dorin, stating that she was residing in a hut close to Seetapore, soliciting money and assistance, and reporting the murder of her husband. Numbers of gun-barrels and locks were brought in from the old magazine, where a great quantity of crowsfeet were found, and ordered to be brought in to-morrow. Behind Mr. Ommanney's house, a very large battery was commenced by Lieutenant Hutchinson. Quantities of grass and stores were brought in.

June 26th – This morning Sir Henry Lawrence, accompanied by his staff, as usual inspected the principal buildings in the vicinity of the Muchee Bhawun and the new round tower, at which great progress had been made, and in which not less than 300 coolies were at work. Proceeding thence he inspected the newly completed defences. opposite the Kolwallee. On his return, Sir H. Lawrence received a letter from Major

Entrance to Lucknow

Raikes at Mynpoorie, giving intelligence of the capture of the city of Delhi on the 13th instant (this afterwards turned out to be a false report). A royal salute was ordered to be fired from the Residency, Muchee Bhawun, and cantonments, and a *feu-de-joie* was fired by the Irregulars, who were quartered in the Dowlut Khana, under the command of Brigadier Gray. Many useful stores, consisting of unwrought materials, rope, and platforms, were brought in from the old magazine. Considerable progress was made in a new battery for heavy guns, which had been commenced in the rear of Mr. Ommanney's house.

In the afternoon, a letter, dated June 23rd, was received from Colonel Neil, commanding at Allahabad, reporting all well there; that 750 Europeans had arrived, and that 1000 more would be with him on the next day; that every effort was being made to despatch 400

38 THE DEFENCE OF LUCKNOW

Europeans, two guns, and 300 Seikhs to Cawnpore, but that much difficulty was experienced in procuring carriage.

Also, at sunset, a letter was received from Sir H. M. Wheeler, K.C.B., dated the 24th instant, detailing his losses, and giving an account of the outbreak, and stating that he had supplies for only eight or ten days at the farthest. His letter was replied to at once, and he was informed by Sir Henry Lawrence of the news received from Allahabad, and also that in ten days at the farthest he would receive aid from Allahabad, and that he must husband his resources as much as possible; that the force at Lucknow was threatened by an attack from eight or ten regiments, three or four of which were within twenty miles.

A reward of one lac of rupees was offered this day for the capture, within a week, dead or alive, of the Nana, at Cawnpore, and means were taken to have the proclamation widely disseminated. With the larger battery commenced to the south, behind Mr. Ommanney's house, we had three large batteries in progress, and were also busily employed in destroying, as far as possible, any buildings that might give cover in the vicinity. Five or six elephants were in course of training to drag heavy guns, so as to enable us to move out without delay, should circumstances require a heavy gun to be taken out.

27th June – This morning a letter from Lieutenant Burnes, Adjutant of the 10th Regiment Oude Irregular Infantry, late at Seetapore, was received. It gave an account of the mutiny at that place, and of the escape of himself, Sir M. Jackson, Bart., and sisters (one of whom had been carried off for some days by the sepoys and brought back), and some others, to a place called

JUNE 27–28th 1857

Mitowlee, where they claimed and received the protection (charily given) of a rajah: they were then all in the jungles, suffering the *greatest* hardships. It also mentioned the safety of another party with Captain Hearsey; who, however, were also in the jungles. Many of these seem to have had the most hair-breadth escapes. No rain had yet fallen, and the heat was most oppressive. The cholera had abated during the past few days, but several cases of smallpox had, however, occurred. The river was reported to have fallen a foot since yesterday.

A report was in circulation early in the day, that General Wheeler had made terms with 'the Nana,' at Cawnpore; but few believed it, and in the evening it was reported incorrect, as heavy firing had been heard yesterday at Cawnpore from Bunnee. Three boxes of crow's feet and a great number of musket-barrels and unwrought stores were brought in from the old magazine at the Dowlut Khana; also a very large quantity of gun carriage-wheels. The force at Nawabgunge was said to be increasing, but very undecided as to what to do. A great force of coolies were at work, and much progress was made in the defences at Muchee Bhawun and the Residency.

28th June – This morning, at about 3 a.m., we had a heavy fall of rain, which continued with slight intervals till 7 a.m. Sir Henry Lawrence proceeded to Hosainabad and examined the defensive preparations made there; returning by the Muchee Bhawun, he found that the buildings occupied by the 32nd had hardly leaked at all. Divine service was performed in the City Hospital (brigade mess), occupied by the officers of the 7th Cavalry, 13th, 48th, and 71st Native Infantry, at 7 a.m. Spies stated that the 17th Regiment Native Infantry,

40 THE DEFENCE OF LUCKNOW

numbering between 250 and 300 men, had gone with five lacs of rupees to Onao on the Cawnpore road – it was believed with the intention of proceeding to Cawnpore.

It having been reported that there were many jewels and valuables in the king's palace, which might fall into the hands of the mutineers, a party under Major Banks, consisting of fifty of the 13th, twenty Seikhs 71st Native Infantry, and the European Volunteer Cavalry, were sent out to fetch them in; which they did about 6 p.m., and reported that they had discovered a large gun.

About 7 p.m. three different natives brought in the very sad and distressing news that the Cawnpore force, having no more ammunition left, had entered into a treaty with their enemies, after which they had all been treacherously murdered, as they embarked in boats to proceed down the river to Allahabad.

Mrs. Dorin, wife of Lieutenant Dorin, who lately commanded the 10th Regiment Oude Irregular Forces, arrived this evening in a country cart, disguised as a native, and accompanied by some clerks. She was for very many days secreted in a village close to Seetapore, and her escape is wonderful. The Serjeant-Major's wife of the 9th Regiment Oude Irregular Infantry also arrived in a doolie, severely wounded. From 8 to 10 o'clock p.m. it rained heavily. A letter, dated the 21st June, received from Benares from Mr. Gubbins, giving an account of the number of Europeans coming up the country, and describing the state of Benares and Allahabad; reporting also an action at Delhi on the 8th instant, when the British troops captured twenty-six guns. News also received from Agra by letter from Captain Nixon, political agent.

June 29th – This morning, a brass gun, a 21-pounder which had been accidentally discovered yesterday by the

JUNE 29th 1857

party who had been despatched under Major Banks, to bring in valuables from the palace (called the 'Kiser Bagh,') was brought in, carriage and waggon all completely ready for immediate service. Some grape shot and powder, chiefly damaged, was also discovered in an adjacent house.

The people in charge of the palace, without giving a thought to resistance as it was at first expected they might do, nevertheless showed an evident reluctance to give information where the arms, &c. were stored. However, it came out at last, that there were more arms within the palace, and a party was despatched to secure them. Seven cart-loads were brought in; chiefly flint muskets, with a few spears, &c.: 4 small guns were also discovered and brought in.

A small party of volunteers, cavalry (twelve men including officers), were sent along the Cawnpore road to bring in information. After going some twelve miles, they returned, having learnt that there were some two or three regiments not far off them. Captain Forbes, with the Seikh Cavalry, was sent off at sunrise to patrol the Nawabgunge road. Six men were also sent on the Sultanpore road to gain information. Both the parties returned at sunset, Captain Forbes bringing intelligence that the enemy were at Chinât, nine miles off.

Our defences progressed, but labour was not so easy to procure as it had been some days before.

* * * * *

The enemy being in strength so near, it was deemed advisable to withdraw the troops from cantonments, which was quietly done at sunset; and it being expected that the enemy would march on Lucknow, Sir Henry Lawrence thought it advisable to move out with a strong force, hoping to meet and oppose them before they

42 THE DEFENCE OF LUCKNOW

entered the suburbs of the city. In order to prevent any notice reaching the enemy of the intended movement, the orders were not given out publicly till 3 o'clock on the following morning, and at the same hour twenty Seikhs under Lieutenant Birch were to be sent to the Iron Bridge, in order to prevent any one crossing over with intelligence of the movement to the enemy.

June 30th – Pursuant to orders, a force, comprising 150 of the 32nd from the Muchee Bhawun, 130 of the 13th Native Infantry, forty Seikhs of the 13th Native Infantry, the 48th, numbering fifty bayonets, the European cavalry thirty-six strong, the Oude Irregular Cavalry, about ninety men, four of the guns of Kaye's battery (Europeans), two of Alexander's guns (natives), two of Bryce's guns (natives), and an eight-inch howitzer, found in the town a few days ago, and which was drawn by two elephants, assembled at the iron bridge at 5.45 a.m. The advance guard was composed of twenty five Seikh Cavalry, and fifteen European Cavalry; twenty Seikh Infantry, and twenty of the 32nd Regiment, the whole under the command of Captain Stevens of the 32nd Foot.

The eight-inch howitzer, two guns of Alexander's battery, two of Kaye's battery, the 13th Native Infantry, two of Bryce's guns, and the detachment of the 32nd Foot, formed the main body, and marched in the above order. The rear guard was composed of the 48th Native Infantry, under Colonel Palmer; the whole force being under the personal command of Sir Henry Lawrence. It was the Brigadier-General's original intention only to proceed to the end of the Pucka road, to the village of Kocaralee; and on their arrival there, our force was halted, and the Brigadier-General, with the advanced

JUNE 30–JULY 1st 1857

guard, proceeded about a mile to the front, whence no one was to be seen. The force was on the point of being ordered to return, when it was decided to make a further reconnaissance; and soon after the enemy were fallen in with, in overwhelming numbers, and the force was compelled to retire with the loss of the eight-inch howitzer, and three 9-pounders.

The enemy came boldly on, and invested us on all sides, firing from all the houses round, which they rapidly loopholed; they also erected a hasty battery for the eight-inch howitzer across the river, from which they threw several well-directed shells; and they began to collect boats for a bridge across the river, the iron bridge being under fire from the Redan.

July 1st – The enemy threw in a very heavy fire of musketry all day and night. Early in the morning they advanced to attack, but were repulsed on all sides with considerable loss from our shells, guns, and musketry. Mr. McRae, of the Civil Engineers Department, and Lieutenant Dashwood, 48th Native Infantry, were wounded, while assisting in working an 18-pounder in the Post Office Battery.

During the day attempts were made to get messengers to cross over to the Muchee Bhawun fort; two or three men started, but as their success was very doubtful, it was determined to work the telegraph on the top of the Residency. This had been previously arranged by the engineer in concert with one on the Muchee Bhawun; it simply consisted of one post with a bar at the top, from which were suspended in one row black stuffed bags, each having its own pulley to work it. After having attracted the attention of the Muchee Bhawun Garrison, the greatest difficulty was found in working the

44 THE DEFENCE OF LUCKNOW

telegraph, from various causes; the chief of which was the tremendous fire which the enemy opened on the spot directly they saw our people on the flat open roof of the Residency. It rained rifle balls, principally from the top of the jail, and some few of the ropes of the bags were actually cut by them; then the pulleys went wrong, and twice the whole machine had to be taken down, and after readjustment put up again. After three hours' hard work under a broiling sun and a heavy fire, the transfer of messages was at last completed.

The message was simply an order to blow up the place and come to the Residency at 12 p.m., bringing the treasure and guns, and destroying as much as possible all spare ammunition. The night was anxiously looked for, as the retreat of the retiring force might he intercepted, and the enemy had the advantage of position. To help the movement, the Brigadier-General gave orders that shortly before 12 p.m., the different mortars and guns from our batteries should open fire, in order to distract the attention of the enemy. This was carried out; especially towards the iron bridge, by which the force must pass.

The movement was most successfully performed; and so quick and noiseless was the march, that at 12.15 the head of the column was at the Lower Water Gate. Here there was some little delay, as the force not being so quickly expected, the gates had not been opened. A very serious accident had nearly happened in consequence of this, for the leading men, finding the gates closed, shouted out 'Open the gates,' and the artillerymen at the guns above, which, loaded with grape, covered the entrance, mistook the words for 'Open with grape,' and were already at the guns, when an officer put them right. The whole force came in without a shot being fired.

JULY 1–2nd 1857

The explosion had not yet taken place; but soon, a shake of the earth, a volume of fire, a terrific report, and an immense mass of black smoke shooting far up into the air, announced to Lucknow, that 240 barrels of gunpowder, and 594,000 rounds of ball and gun ammunition, had completed the destruction of Muchee Bhawun, which we had with so much labour provisioned and fortified.

July 2nd – Arrangements were made for posting and stationing the Muchee Bhawun force which came in last night, and placing the field-pieces in position; all of which Sir H. Lawrence himself personally superintended. About 8 a.m. Sir Henry returned to the Residency, and, being much fatigued, laid down on his bed. Soon after an eight-inch shell from the eight-inch howitzer of the enemy, entered the room at the window, and exploding, a fragment struck the Brigadier-General on the upper part of the right thigh near the hip, inflicting a fearful wound. Captain Wilson, who was standing alongside the bed with one knee on it at the time, reading a memorandum to Sir Henry, was knocked down by falling bricks and slightly wounded in the back by a piece of shell. Sir H. Lawrence's nephew, Mr. Lawrence, had an equally narrow escape, being on another bed close by: he was not hurt; the fourth individual in the room was a native servant, who lost one of his feet by a fragment of the shell. It was at once pronounced that Sir Henry Lawrence's wound was mortal, and his sufferings were great. He immediately sent for Major Banks, and appointed him to succeed him as Chief-Commissioner, and appointed Colonel Inglis to command the troops. He was then removed to Dr. Fayrer's house, which was somewhat less under fire.

Lucknow from the balcony of the Residency

About noon this day, a round shot came into a room on the lower story of the residency, and shattered the thigh of Miss Palmer (daughter of Colonel Palmer, 48th Regiment, Native Infantry) so dreadfully, that instant amputation was obliged to be resorted to. All the garrison were greatly grieved, and the Natives much dispirited at our severe loss, in that popular and very distinguished officer, Sir Henry Lawrence.

A perfect hurricane of jinjal, round shot, and musketry all day and all night. Probably not less than 10,000 men fired into our position from the surrounding houses; the balls fell in showers, and hardly any place was safe from them. Many of the garrison were hit in places which, before the siege, it was considered would be perfectly safe; but the enemy fired some of them from a great distance out of the town, from the tops of high houses, and the balls fell everywhere.

*

JULY 3rd 1857

July 3rd – It is difficult to chronicle the proceedings of these few days, for everywhere confusion reigned supreme. That unfortunate day of Chinât precipitated everything, inasmuch as we were closely shut up several days before anything of the kind was anticipated. People had made no arrangements for provisioning themselves: many indeed never dreamt of such a necessity; and the few that had were generally too late. Again, many servants were shut out the first day, and all attempts to approach us were met by a never-ceasing fusilade. But though they could not get in, they succeeded in getting out; and after a few days, those who could boast of servants or attendants of any kind formed a very small and envied minority. The servants in many instances eased their masters of any superfluous article of value, easy of carriage. In fact, the confusion can be better imagined than described.

The head of the Commissariat had, most unfortunately for the garrison, received a severe wound at Chinât, which effectually deprived them of his valuable aid. His office was all broken up; his goomastahs and baboos were not with us, and the officers appointed to assist him were all new hands. Besides all this, the first stores opened were approachable only by one of the most exposed roads, and very many of the camp followers preferred going without food to the chance of being shot. Some did not know where to apply, so that for three or four days, many went without rations; and this in no small degree added to the number of desertions. Owing to these desertions, the commissariat and battery bullocks had no attendants to look after them, and went wandering all over the place looking for food; they tumbled into wells, were shot down in numbers by the enemy, and added greatly to the labour which fell on the

48 THE DEFENCE OF LUCKNOW

garrison, as fatigue parties of civilians and officers, after being in the defences all day repelling the enemy's attack, were often employed six and seven hours burying cattle killed during the day, and which from the excessive heat became offensive in a few hours. The artillery and other horses were everywhere to be seen loose, fighting and tearing at one another, driven mad for want of food and water; the garrison being too busily employed in the trenches to be able to secure them.

Poor Sir H. Lawrence suffered somewhat less to-day, but was sinking fast, and at times his mind wandered. A tremendous fire all day, more particularly on the Baillie Guard and Dr. Fayrer's house where Sir Henry was lying. We thus early in the siege learnt that all our proceedings inside were known (through some party or other) to our enemies. Miss Palmer died to-day, and Mr. Ommanney of the Civil Service, was dangerously wounded under the ear by a grape shot, while in the Redan battery.

July 4th – A tremendous fire all night; but no effort was made to storm our position. To the great grief of our garrison, Sir Henry Lawrence died this morning about 8 o'clock, from the effects of his wound. Shortly before his death, Mr. G. H. Lawrence while standing in the front verandah of Dr. Fayrer's house, was wounded by a musket-ball through his right shoulder.

At night, there was a great uproar in the city, which evidently underwent a thorough plundering. Notwithstanding this, the same heavy fire was kept up throughout the night. Every one at work trying to throw up some shelter for himself. In the course of the day, a 9-pounder, brought by the insurgents and placed behind a small mosque close to our furthest water-gate, was

JULY 4–7th 1857 49

spiked by a private of the 32nd and four others from Innes's post, who shot four of the enemy. The enemy were taken by surprise while at their dinner.

July 5th – From 2 till 6 o'clock a.m., heavy rain; and extremely heavy firing all day. Several casualties among our garrison. A soldier of the 32nd was said to have killed five men in ten shots from the Cawnpore battery, which was subjected to a very severe musketry fire. Continued efforts were made to collect all the horses and secure them, but it was impossible to do anything during the day. The fire was so heavy, and the night was so dark, it was difficult to get hold of the animals, who were half mad; added to which four or five horses were killed daily, which had to be buried at night by parties of officers, who, after being exposed to a fearful sun in the trenches all day, were often out in the rain till 12 and 1 o'clock in the morning, engaged in burying horses and bullocks, in order to prevent the dreadful stench which would otherwise have been increased, and which had already become almost insupportable.

July 6th – The usual amount of musketry and cannon fire all the morning: about 2 o'clock in the afternoon it became very severe, especially towards the Baillie Guard, which seemed the favourite point to-day for the heaviest fire. A heavy cannonade heard about three miles off for about half an hour. About 4 p.m. the flashes of the guns were distinctly seen. The cause was unknown. The enemy digging trenches in all directions. The carriage of one of our 9-pounders was disabled by the enemy.

July 7th – A heavy fire all the morning.
A sortie was made by fifty of the 32nd and twenty

50 THE DEFENCE OF LUCKNOW

Sikhs, led by Captain Lawrence, Captain Mansfield, Ensign Green, 13th Native Infantry, and Ensign Studdy, – the latter led. The storming took place at noon. The object was to examine M. Johannes's house, and discover if the enemy were driving mines: it was perfectly successful, and fifteen or twenty of the enemy were killed. Our loss was one Seikh and one 32nd slightly, and one 32nd severely wounded.

This afternoon a very sad event occurred. Major Francis, 13th Native Infantry, who had commanded at the Muchee Bhawun, and who was in command of the brigade mess square, was struck in the legs by a round shot, which completely fractured both legs, rendering amputation of one *immediate,* and great fears were entertained for the other. He was a brave, good officer, and much respected by all, and one in whom Sir Henry Lawrence had much confidence. The calm manner in which he bore his misfortune, gained him the sympathies of all. Not a murmur escaped him; his only anxiety being a hope that the authorities would bear testimony that he had performed his duty. The Rev. Mr. Polehampton, military chaplain, was severely wounded in the side this day, by a rifle ball, while in hospital. One of the walls of the Racket Court, now used as a bhoosa gadown, fell in, and a quantity of the bhoosa became exposed in consequence. All spare tarpaulings were immediately supplied to cover it, and officers and men worked hard for two hours, in a deluge of rain. The rains, so long expected, seem now fairly set in. It commenced raining heavily at 2 p.m., and continued pouring down the whole night.

July 8th – All very much as usual, and very heavy rain fell, which somewhat abated the enemy's fire. Every effort was made to put the place in some kind of order and to feed the bullocks.

Poor Major Francis insensible and sinking: he died at 7 p.m., and was buried by a party of officers close to Mr. Ommanney's grave. Every effort was made to curtail the expenditure of provision, and officers were placed on half rations every third day. Very few servants remained, and most of the officers had none. All were on duty thirteen and twenty hours a day; and constant alarms took place at night, rendering it necessary for all to stand to their arms. Fears were entertained of the bhoosa stack taking fire, as the outer wall of the Racket Court had fallen down and left it exposed. All available officers and men worked hard, in heavy rain, to get it covered in again with tarpaulins. Twelve Seikhs of the 13th Native Infantry deserted last night. All the Hindoos and Mussulmans of the 13th, 48th, and 71st behaved nobly.

July 9th – Much rain fell during the morning. About 4 a.m. the enemy made an attack on the Baillie Guard Gate, and about 300 showed themselves, shouting and sounding the 'Advance,' on the bugle; but being received with a few rounds of grape, and a steady fire from the 13th, they speedily disappeared. Very much the same thing occurred soon after at the Cawnpore battery. Continued firing all day.

This was now the tenth day of the siege, and the heavy musketry fire on every side had never for an instant ceased night or day; and at times the fire was terrific. Many casualties occurred, and our want of protection at the different crossings over from one side of the Residency compound to the other, was very much felt. To-day, an excellent soldier, and a man greatly respected, Mr. Bryson, formerly Serjeant-major of the 16th

52 THE DEFENCE OF LUCKNOW

Lancers, was shot through the head, while endeavouring to strengthen his post. The enemy appeared to have had some excellent marksmen. The commissariat began to work well, and all were well supplied. The officers were placed, however, on half rations every third day as a precautionary measure. Lieutenant Dashwood of the 48th Native Infantry, died of cholera after a few hours' illness.

July 10th – This morning the enemy's fire was continued much as usual. A sepoy of the 13th was killed early in the morning, and later in the day a private of the 32nd Foot and an artilleryman were wounded. The horses of the cavalry and the artillery, which, during the first days of the siege, were loose and driven nearly mad from hunger and thirst, galloping about and creating the greatest confusion, had now been nearly all turned out, though not without much trouble; and fifty of the best were retained, and secured in the Seikh square. All the bullocks were now also secured, and arrangements made for feeding and watering them; but numbers of horses and bullocks died, and their burial at night by working parties, in addition to nightly fatigue parties for the purpose of burying the dead, carrying up supplies from exposed positions, repairing entrenchments, draining, and altering the position of guns, in addition to attending on the wounded, caused excessive fatigue to the thin garrison, who had but little rest night or day: there were few officers with more than one servant, and one third certainly had *none*. In all duties, the officers equally shared the labours with the men, carrying loads and digging pits for putrid animals, at night, in heavy rain. All exerted themselves to the utmost, alternately exposed to a burning sun and heavy rain. Towards the

JULY 10–11th 1857 53

middle of the day, the enemy fired less than they had previously done on any occasion since the siege commenced.

We received no news from any quarter, but sent off many letters. Every exertion was made to grind up the wheat in store by hand-mills; and this day thirteen maunds and two seers were ground. The firing towards the afternoon to-day was very slack, comparatively speaking. There was a comparatively slight cannonade. An injured 9-pounder in the Cawnpore battery was removed by us and replaced by another.

July 11th – About 1 o'clock this morning the whole force stood to their arms, in consequence of some information which was received, reporting that an attack was immediately intended. The force remained prepared till daylight, when, as usual, a smart firing on all sides began. An artilleryman was killed at Captain Simmons's battery. The enemy fired several round shot, and were most persevering in keeping us on the alert, and worrying us as much as possible. Their fire had never yet ceased day or night: sometimes it was heavier than at others, but it never abated altogether on any side.

At night the officers buried a horse which had died close to the brigade square; the night was intensely hot and close, and the labour was excessive: – the horse having died on the Pucka road, had to be dragged to a considerable distance before a grave could be dug. A great many of the stores were also brought up from the church by the assistance of a fatigue party of officers, who had all the carts to load and unload. Two of the 32nd Foot were killed during the night, which passed off with a heavy fire.

*

54 THE DEFENCE OF LUCKNOW

July 12th – The heat still excessive, and the fatigue of the garrison was *very* great. Enemy were most persevering, and loopholed every place within fifty or sixty yards of our defences. They were evidently determined to do their best to get into the position, and had closed in on every side. We had no intelligence from any quarter; for though we had sent out many messengers, not one returned.

About 8 o'clock in the evening the enemy made an attempt to attack the Baillie Gate; but fell back, on being received with shells and musketry. About 12 p.m. they renewed their efforts on Mr. Gubbins's side with similar effect. They repeatedly sounded the advance, and were frequently heard abusing each other for not advancing. In half an hour they retired, and for the rest of the night they contented themselves with a heavy fire on the Cawnpore battery.

July 13th – The heat was dreadful, and garrison were greatly fatigued. The enemy reoccupied Johannes's house, and fired smartly down the street, killing two sepoys and wounding a conductor: they also pushed close up under the Redan, and greatly annoyed our outposts. Lieutenant Charlton of the 32nd Foot was shot through the head in the church, and very dangerously wounded. Several shells were fired into Johannes's house, and the walls of the house opposite to it were loopholed. Nevertheless we could not dislodge them, and they annoyed us greatly. The Havildar-major of the 13th was wounded through the thigh to-day.

The enemy possessed many excellent marksmen, and fired so many shots from every point that it was exceedingly dangerous to be seen anywhere, even for an instant: they fired several logs of wood bound with iron,

JULY 13–14th 1857

and were evidently at this period hard up for round shot. In the evening they fired several carcases, and succeeded once in setting the Residency on fire; but it was soon extinguished. All the European officers laboured hard to get the supplies out of the church.

July 14th – Heavy rain, thunder and lightning, and night intensely dark. No alarms, and less firing than usual. Heavy rain at daybreak, which cleared off at 9 o'clock, when the enemy assembled in force. They were apparently undecided how to act, for they moved about in various directions, and in about half an hour retired altogether; but they fired many carcases, shot, and logs of wood shod with iron, and displayed several new batteries. We threw up a traverse near the Post-office gate, in order to save our people from the fire from Johannes's house, which was very sharp. Our sharp-shooters killed four of the enemy in Johannes's house. Four Seikhs of the 13th deserted, leaving their arms and accoutrements. Still no information of any kind.

Enemy erecting new batteries; one of which opened about 5 p.m. with a 9-pounder on the gable end of the brigade mess, occupied by the ladies and children, and the roof of which was held by a party of officers, assisted by six men of the 32nd. At the first discharge, a soldier of the 32nd had his thigh fractured, rendering amputation necessary. They fired several iron shot, which tore away the parapet; but fortunately no one else was hurt. The night was very dark, and the enemy fired a great deal; more particularly on Mr. Gubbins's post, where Lieutenant Lester was mortally wounded: towards daylight the fire abated. Several cases of cholera. The enemy's fire today destroyed a 9-pounder of ours, smashing the axle tree all to pieces.

Seikh Cavalryman

July 15th – The enemy opened fire from their 9-pounder battery, situated about fifty yards from the end of the brigade mess, and fired many shots; but the garrison laid close, and up to 3 p.m. no casualties occurred. Towards the middle of the day, the enemy's fire lulled to a greater extent than it had ever done since the siege commenced.

The stores out of Anderson's house got in; the house being entirely destroyed by round shot; though still nobly held by the garrison. A mortar moved down to the gate of the Post-office, behind the traverse, and several shells were thrown into Johannes's house. All much as usual. The enemy fired three rounds of grape into the Redan battery during the night, but fortunately hit no one.

July 16th – The heat during the night was fearful. A slight alarm about 2 a.m., but it was soon over. The

JULY 16–17th 1857

enemy fired smartly throughout the night, and in the morning sent several round shot through the roof of the brigade mess, and hit the Residency. They were busy, besides, making batteries in the garden of Johannes's house, and opposite the 13th and the Cawnpore battery.

We shelled the enemy heavily during the forenoon, throwing them far into the town and across the river. Lieutenant Bryce was badly wounded in the thigh early this morning; and later in the day, Lieutenant O'Brien of the 84th was shot through the arm. In the evening the enemy kept up a heavy fusilade, and we shelled them smartly; they fired a shell which narrowly escaped falling into our bhoosa stack. At half-past 11 o'clock, they fired a good deal on the Cawnpore battery, and made a feint of attacking, but finding us well on the alert did not do so. Our wheat-grinding operations continued, and we now had hand-mills sufficiently well worked to grind twenty maunds of atta daily. During the night we threw up a stockade and traverse, as a protection against the musketry which swept the entrance of the Residency.

July 17th – The heat excessive. A very heavy fire during the night, and the garrison kept on the alert, preventing rest and greatly fatiguing all. Several cases of cholera and deaths of children occurred. Twenty-two maunds of wheat were ground.

To-day a bad accident occurred: Lieutenant Alexander, of the Artillery, and Captain Barlow, 50th Native Infantry, in firing a mortar, were most severely burnt by the piece going off at the time of loading. The enemy sent two shells into the Residency which exploded, but fortunately caused no loss of life. The stench from putrid animals was most offensive. Painful boils about the head

58 THE DEFENCE OF LUCKNOW

were very prevalent. The wounded doing well. The prisoners and main guard removed to another place, in order to give more room at the hospital.

The enemy were busy making more batteries and intrenchments. In the night about 12 o'clock, the enemy made an attack on Mr. Gubbins's position, but were received with a steady fire, and soon driven back.

July 18th – Rain began falling about 4 a.m. and continued to do so till 8 a.m., when the heat became insufferable. The enemy fired several round shot, which hit the brigade mess; and they also took up an annoying position in one of the towers which remained of the Ferad Buksh gate. They were, however, speedily dislodged by a few exceedingly well-directed shots from Lieutenant Bonham, from an 18-pounder in the Post-office. Two children died of cholera. In the evening the enemy fired many round shot into the Post-office, Dr. Fayrer's, Mr. Gubbins's and the brigade mess house: they evidently had been reinforced in guns. At night, Brigadier Inglis, Captain Wilson, Lieutenant Innes, and Ensign Birch, proceeded to the gate with eight Europeans, and dragged in a body that was seen lying near the gate, and which it was supposed might be the body of one of our spies shot coming in. It was safely brought in, and found to be the corpse of a woman. Nothing was found on the body. The enemy got into the turret on the top of Mr. Johannes's house, and fired into the Cawnpore battery: fortunately no casualties occurred, and the night, which was fearfully oppressive, passed away with a heavy fire from the enemy.

July 19th – Dreadful heat: cloudy, but no rain. Enemy fired round shot all the morning. About half-past 9 a large shot passed through a room in the Residency, in which the officers were at breakfast, fracturing the leg of Lieutenant Harmer, 32nd Foot, but providentially injuring no one else; about the same time Lieutenant Arthur, 7th Cavalry, was shot dead (through the heart) in the Cawnpore battery. Our 18-pounder fired several shots, and we threw several shells. The enemy seemed to be at work at the Muchee Bhawun, probably looking for shot which had been buried in the ruins.

About 12 o'clock to-day the enemy sounded the advance, and threatened an attack on the Redan. A few shells, however, soon made them give up all idea of coming on. They got into Johannes's house in force, and fired steadily into the cook-house of the brigade mess.

Much drunkenness prevailed amongst a few of the garrison, who had stolen quantities of liquor, which could not be discovered. From the commencement of the siege, the large quantities of liquor in the hands of the merchants caused much anxiety, and every possible endeavour was made to get it all into safe custody. One or two alarms during the early part of the night. Mr. Polehampton (wounded and in hospital) died this day from cholera.

July 20th – From midnight the enemy remained unusually quiet, and at daylight all seemed much as usual. About half-past 8 a.m. it was reported that a very large body of men could be seen marching about in different directions within a few hundred yards of our position. A sharp look-out was kept, and the garrison stood to their arms. At a quarter-past 10, the enemy sprung a mine inside the water gate, and about twenty-five yards from our inner defences: the explosion was great, and was evidently intended to have blown up our

60 THE DEFENCE OF LUCKNOW

Redan battery, and also to act as a signal; for immediately the dust and smoke subsided, a very heavy fire of round shot was commenced from every gun that the enemy possessed, followed immediately almost by a terrific fire of musketry, under which the enemy made an attempt to storm the Redan and Innes's house. The garrison were ready, and every one at his post, and the attack was coolly met and repulsed; however the enemy advanced boldly and came up within twenty-five yards of the battery in immense force, but were unable to withstand the fire of our men.

They made a similar attempt on Innes's house, but were similarly repulsed by the garrison, consisting of twelve men of the 32nd, twelve of the 13th Native Infantry, and a few uncovenanted gentlemen, under Ensign Loughnan (who distinguished himself greatly): very great loss was inflicted on the enemy, who repeatedly tried to advance, but were driven back each time with much slaughter. Finding their efforts useless, the enemy fell back, and contented themselves with throwing in a terrific storm of musketry; from which we shielded our men as much as possible, by keeping them laid under our defences. Almost at the same time an attack was made on the Cawnpore Battery, but the enemy's standard-bearer (who advanced bravely) being shot in the ditch of the battery, the rest fell back. The enemy now moved towards Lieutenant Anderson's house and Captain Germon's post, with scaling-ladders, but were well received and fell back with much loss. The attack was now over, though for the rest of the day, until 4 p.m., the enemy threw in a heavy fire; when it gradually subsided: the attack was mostly confined to the points above noted.

In the afternoon they succeeded in making a lodgment

in some pucka cook-houses inside our abattis, and began
to use a crowbar, which was distinctly heard. We made a
hole through to them from above, through which they
fired, injuring no one; but on our throwing down some
hand grenades, they fled across the road, two being shot
by the officers who were watching from above. The 13th,
71st, and 48th sepoys all behaved well, and the manner
in which the outposts were held, was beyond all praise.
The uncovenanted distinguished themselves greatly. We
had fortunately only four men killed, and some twelve
wounded: Captain Forbes, Lieutenant Grant, Lieutenant
Edmonstone, and Mr. Hely, were wounded. All were
under arms from eight in the morning until eight at
night, and greatly fatigued and worn out.

July 21st – All very quiet during the night. The enemy
were probably fatigued with their exertions yesterday,
for throughout the night only a few round shot were
thrown in. About 10 a.m. the enemy lodged themselves
in some force in the low buildings between the Seikh
courtyard and Mr. Gubbins's post, but were driven out by
a few shells, and were fired on by the officers of the
brigade mess, as they ran across a small lane: they did
not attempt to reoccupy the position during the day.
About 12 o'clock, Major Banks was killed by a musket-
shot through the head, as he was reconnoitring from the
top of an outhouse. Mr. Gubbins's garrison was fired on
smartly during the morning, and many round shot were
sent into Mr. Gubbins's house; the garrison of which had
many alarms during the day. Painful boils very
prevalent. A dreadful stench pervaded the place in
consequence of the number of dead horses and bullocks,
which, lying direct under the fire of the enemy, we were
unable to remove. Excessive heat, and several cases of

62 THE DEFENCE OF LUCKNOW

cholera. Great fatigue; no news. Poor Dr. Brydon severely wounded in Mr. Gubbins's house. Two Europeans killed, and two wounded; also one of the 13th sepoys.

July 22nd – Very heavy rain began to fall at 1 a.m., and continued till 8 a.m., when it cleared off. During the heavy rain, the enemy only fired slightly. After 8 a.m. it became more brisk, and they fired several round shot, but were not very active during the forenoon. Cholera still prevalent. Our numerical strength much diminished, as we had had 151 casualties in the 32nd Regiment alone. The enemy moved the 8-inch howitzer from its old position, and brought it across the river by elephants, with a tumbril behind it. Up to this date, we had no intelligence of any kind from any quarter, and, indeed, we had received none since the 27th ultimo. Many messengers were sent with letters, but not a single line did we receive in reply. A letter was sent off to Cawnpore to-day, and conveyed by a man named Ram Singh, a Seikh subadar of the 63rd Native Infantry. The enemy steadily loop-holing all the houses close round about, and evidently up to some new attempt at our position.

At dusk heavy rain; we got out a strong working party, and opened our large powder magazine, and after much labour and exertion got up 150 barrels out of the 240 we had buried. The night was pitch dark, and the rain fell heavily, and the work being outside of our entrenchment, over which all the barrels had to be handed out of mud knee deep, rendered the work fearfully fatiguing. Many of the officers and civilians worked for five hours at this work. Only a few shots during the night. Boils still very prevalent. A Seikh from the cavalry deserted. One or two

JULY 22–23rd 1857

cases of cholera. Mortification having set in, Mr. Hely's arm was amputated.

The buildings outside Mr. Gubbins's position were shelled at sunset, and after we had driven the enemy out, we made a sortie through the wall (in which we had cut a large hole), and rushed out and examined the houses in which the enemy had been. We failed to find any trace of mining. We lost one man of the 32nd, killed. Mrs. Dorin was killed dead by a musket ball in Mr. Gubbins's house to-day.

July 23rd – Very heavy rain during the night. About 2 a.m. the enemy sounded the 'turn out', and at 3 the 'assembly'. About 1 a.m. a native pensioner, who left us on the 27th to gain information, came in, and said he had been confined by the enemy thirteen days, but had been to Cawnpore and left it two days ago, that a British force with twelve guns was there; that they had fought three times with the Nana's troops, and had completely beaten them, taking many guns, and that they were crossing the river preparatory to advancing to our assistance. He stated that he had not brought a letter, for fear of being detained by the enemy; he vouched to the truth of his statement, declined a pecuniary reward, and was urgent to go back quickly while it rained heavily and all was quiet comparatively. He left in two hours, taking a small note for the officer commanding the forces.

At daylight there were fewer of the enemy than we had yet seen about, and those less active; though they still fired smartly all around. Stench from dead animals in some parts dreadful; as we had very few servants of any kind and our fighting men were so few and so harassed, that we were helpless to bury them. Heavy showers both day and night, keeping the garrison constantly drenched

64 THE DEFENCE OF LUCKNOW

to the skin, and making all most uncomfortable; particularly as few had a change of clothes. Enemy fired slackly during the afternoon. Cannonaded their bridge of boats, which was broken by our 18-pounder shot. Several cases of small-pox. Sick and wounded much crowded. The upper story of the hospital being under fire of round shot, the wounded were, from the commencement of the siege, confined to the ground floor, which with difficulty contained their beds. At night it rained hard; and in spite of all difficulties, we succeeded in getting up the remaining ninety barrels of powder, and safely deposited them in the centre of our position. A false alarm about 12 o'clock at night, that the enemy had got into the churchyard.

July 24th – Morning fair and cloudy. The enemy endeavoured to repair the bridge of boats, but were prevented by the fire of our 18-pounder. The heat and stench terrible, and the flies were beyond endurance, contesting every particle of food with us, and preventing all attempts at rest during the day. Only a few round shot thrown, but the enemy actively at work about forty yards from the Redan battery, in a deep trench. Advantage taken of the temporary lull to repair some of our defences, which had sunk a great deal in consequence of the heavy rain; but our men, reduced in numbers and harassed to death day and night, were not capable of any prolonged exertion. Every possible effort was made to grind wheat, and from twenty-five to thirty hand-mills were kept steadily at work, producing an average of twenty maunds of flour daily. The 48th Regiment Native Infantry have had seven, and the 71st Regiment, upwards of fifty desertions, since the commencement of the siege.

Elephants carrying troops to the camp before Lucknow

THE DEFENCE OF LUCKNOW

About dusk, the enemy, for the first time, sent in many shells; which, however, caused no loss, fortunately. The commissariat department busy with the stores, getting ghee up from the Round House; while a fatigue party of officers, under Captain Radcliffe, threw up earth, and heightened the traverse across the road, near the Post-office gate. Lieutenant Hutchinson, of the Engineers, accompanied by Lieutenant Birch, crept down in the dark, and examined, as well as they could, the enemy's works in the immediate vicinity of the Redan. Night dark and cloudy.

July 25th – The night passed away tolerably quietly; the enemy firing several 18-pound shot into the Cawnpore battery. At daylight they were tolerably quiet, contenting themselves with musketry; but about 8 a.m. they fired an 8-inch shell, which fell through the centre of the roof of the Post-office, and lodged on the table on which the officers of that post breakfasted; fortunately it did not explode, and no mischief was done. Immediately after, several shells, apparently thrown out of mortars, were thrown in, and continued to be so during the forenoon. One fell in the verandah of the Post-office, and shattered the hand of an artilleryman. Two men of the 32nd were shot this morning by the enemy's sharp-shooters. Still not one word of intelligence from any quarter, though this was now the twenty-sixth day we had been besieged. We knew nothing; but the most absurd rumours were afloat amongst the natives, and indeed among many of the Europeans, who were credulous enough to believe them. Removed the powder out of the place in which we had it, to a tykhana under the Begum Kotee which the engineers considered safer than where it was first removed to. Very slight firing on the river side, but the enemy still very active near the Redan. Much difference of opinion existed as to the object of the work; the majority believed that they were mining, while the engineers thought they were only making a trench. Although the earlier part of the morning had been quiet enough, towards 11 and 12 o'clock, a very sharp fire was opened and maintained on the side of the Post-office and Cawnpore battery.

The casualties on this side alone amounted to six, besides three others in different places, which made the total of the day's casualties one of the heaviest on record. Towards evening the enemy commenced shelling us. Seven shells were sent in, but did no damage. Opinions differed whether they were discharged from howitzers or mortars.

About 11 p.m. a pensioner, who had been sent out from this on the 22nd instant with a letter, effected his entrance into Mr. Gubbins's compound, and produced a letter which he had brought back from the camp. He was at once brought to Brigadier Inglis and examined. The letter proved to be one from Lieutenant-Colonel Fraser Tytler, Quartermaster-General with General Havelock's force. It was determined to transmit to General Havelock by this man a plan of our position and of the roads approaching it, with memoranda drawn up by the engineers.

July 26th − At daybreak cloudy and sultry: enemy tolerably quiet, but about 8 a.m. they threw in several shells. From 11 to 1 very heavy rain, and a partial cessation from firing, during which Lieutenant Lewin of the Artillery, who was reconnoitring from the Cawnpore battery, was shot dead by one of the enemy's sharp-shooters. Enemy recommenced shelling from the city

68   THE DEFENCE OF LUCKNOW

side: few of them to be seen, all being under cover. Supposed to be mining at the Cawnpore battery. A countermine commenced by us, out of the house next the battery; but having no workmen except our harassed soldiers, the work was slow; however, as the engineers seemed to entertain little or no doubt but that the enemy were mining, it was necessary to endeavour to counteract them. Little musketry fire during the afternoon; the enemy throwing in heavy shot, fired at a great elevation (apparently out of howitzer). One or two cases of cholera. Garrison in good spirits at the prospect of early relief.

A letter and plan of our position forwarded at night by a messenger to the officer commanding the relieving force: 5000 rupees promised the messenger if he brought a reply. Suddenly at 10 p.m. the enemy commenced a heavy fire along the whole of the city front of our position; but nothing came of it, as after a few shells had been thrown amongst them, their fire gradually subsided, and all became tolerably quiet again. During this heavy firing, a sad accident occurred; Lieutenant Shepherd of the 7th Cavalry being shot dead in the brigade square, by a shot fired from the top of the brigade mess by one of our garrison. This was the only casualty of the night.

July 27th – From midnight all quiet, save the usual musketry fire. Cloudy, sultry weather. About 7 a.m. two planks were observed laid across the road in front of Johannes's house. They were not seen the night before, and being carefully watched, a man's hand was seen coming up from below; and soon after some eight feet of earth fell in, showing the direction of a mine of the enemy right across the road, and pointing direct for our stockade, within six feet of which it had apparently reached. This was a most fortunate discovery for us: they had

JULY 27–28th 1857

evidently kept this mine too near the surface, and the heavy rain had broke it in. Our mine continued to be pushed on as rapidly as possible, and our sharp-shooters from the top of the brigade mess kept up so hot a fire on the enemy's sap from above, that they could make no attempt to repair the mischief. Much fever prevalent, consequent on being constantly wet day and night

Towards the afternoon, the enemy again covered their trench with boards; but we got a mortar under our wall, and after one or two failures, a shell fell right into the hole and blew all the planks away, leaving the remains of the trench exposed to view giving us no further anxiety. Fine weather in the afternoon. Enemy heard mining towards the brigadier mess; on which a shaft was commenced by the officers, and the enemy ceased working. Late in the evening, the enemy were very distinctly heard mining towards the Seikh lines; on which the Seikhs, under Lieutenant Hardinge, commenced and sunk an eight feet shaft; hearing us, the enemy seemed to stop working. All quiet, with the exception of the usual amount of firing. Fever, diarrhœa, dysentery, and painful boils, from constant wet and exposure, still prevalent amongst the garrison. Mrs. Grant (wife of Lieutenant Grant) died of cholera. Captain Boileau, 7th Cavalry, was wounded to-day.

July 28th – Much shouting and bugling amongst the enemy during the early part of the morning: heavy rain at daylight. Made repairs to the Redan battery, also made a small field work for a 9-pounder. Sickness much increased, and for many days past only one engineer officer was available for duty: hard work, privation, and exposure day and night to wet and heat, few could long stand against. We had no further news of our coming

70 THE DEFENCE OF LUCKNOW

friends, but trusted that to-day they would reach Bunnee.

The enemy threw in several shells, also a number of stink-pots, which were a very curious composition of large pieces of our exploded iron shell sewn up in canvas, and surrounded by flax and resin, with dry powder in the centre: these, from the commencement of the siege, had been thrown in daily from a howitzer; they made a fearful hissing noise and great stench, and finally exploded. They were not very dangerous, unless they exploded *very* close to a person. We also had a few rockets thrown in, but not many; and lately a number of shrapnel shells, fired apparently from a howitzer with a very great elevation. The enemy's miners could now be distinctly heard working close to the Seikh Square sap.

The room in the Residency containing the jewellery and valuables belonging to the late King of Oude, was broken into last night by some of the garrison, and most of them stolen. Enemy tolerably quiet in the afternoon. About 5 p.m. our sap in the Seikh Square, which had been going on as fast as we could push it in the direction of the enemy's, met theirs, which they continued to work to the last moment. On our crowbar, however, going through into their gallery, they instantly fled out of it, and commenced to fill in their shaft. We immediately made use of their gallery, and blew the whole up with 100 lbs. of powder, which brought down all the adjacent houses, &c. After this the enemy tolerably quiet. Good progress made in our Cawnpore sap.

July 29th – A fine moonlight night. Enemy fired many round shot about daylight, and also musketry from the houses across the road; they also threw in many carcases, which nearly all fell in the vicinity of the

JULY 29th 1857

Cawnpore battery. No intelligence. All were anxious for the relieving force, which we thought could not be far off. Our Cawnpore sap loaded with 200lbs. of powder, ready to explode whenever it might be thought most advisable. Colonel Halford, 71st Regiment Native Infantry, who had been long ill, died this morning.

A few convalescents joined the ranks, giving more room in the hospital, which was greatly overcrowded in consequence of all the patients being obliged to be kept on the ground floor, as also the state prisoners and their servants; the round shot passing so frequently through the upper story as to make it impossible to make use of it. Rumour stated that the enemy had gone out in force to meet our coming army, and had left two or three regiments of infantry, and a body of military police, to keep us in; but it was most difficult to tell what force we had opposed to us, as the enemy seldom or never showed in any number, but kept in the houses under cover, occasionally yelling, bugling, and throwing in a heavy fire, then subsiding into the usual steady fire which went on night and day.

Firing of cannon heard in the direction of Cawnpore. We hoped it was our friends. All anxious, but all conjecture. Enemy recommenced mining towards our mine in the Cawnpore battery. About 6 p.m., a heavy firing was heard for about five minutes in the road from Cawnpore, and in about half an hour, several guns were heard in the direction of cantonments; this made us think it was a salute fired by the enemy for some reason or other; probably to reassure themselves. However, all is conjecture; but it threw our garrison into a great state of excitement, and many (indeed most) stoutly maintained it was our force. About 300 or 400 sepoys were seen at the same time running across the iron bridge towards cantonments in great haste. We fired two shots at them with an 18-pounder.

The excitement gradually cooled down; the enemy keeping up their usual fire. Another mine was discovered this evening, by a portion of it falling in: it was running in the direction of Sago's house. Lieutenant Grant of the Bombay army, whose wife and child died a few days ago of cholera, died in hospital this night, from the effects of his wound: his right hand had been blown off by a hand-grenade. A fine moonlight night.

July 30th – From 2 a.m. till daylight heavy rain. Enemy got in close under the wall of the Seikh lines, and began some kind of operations against it; they were so close that no musket could be fired, being under a projecting piece of the wall; they were, however, dislodged by a few pistol shots, and ran off. No further incident occurred during the night, beyond that there was the usual amount of firing into our position, and bugling on the part of the enemy. After daylight enemy fired slackly. Terrible stench in many parts of the garrison from half-buried corpses and animals, which we had no time or means to bury properly. Several cases of fever, cholera, and smallpox.

About 9 a.m. a number of sepoys and matchlockmen were seen coming along the Cawnpore road, and for about an hour and a half a continuous stream of men came in in detached parties of twenty and thirty: some sepoys were among them. Slack firing during the forenoon, only a few shells and musketry. In the afternoon, heavy rain for an hour. Unable to discover what the enemy were about. Considerable progress made in a sap, which we had sunk in an outhouse close to the corner of the brigade mess-house, where most of the children and ladies were located. At first the enemy were heard mining towards us, but since yesterday we had not heard them. We continued, however, to steadily push our sap, hoping either to come across that of the enemy or succeed in getting under Johannes' house; from which they fired all day long on any one who showed himself. Yesterday an artillery sergeant, who incautiously crossed the road commanded from Johannes' house, was shot through both legs. The enemy had many riflemen, and some of them were most expert shots, firing through our loopholes.

About 8 p.m., as Captain Wilson, Lieutenant Barwell, Lieutenant James, and Mr. Lawrence were sitting on the chubootra of the Begum Kotee, a shell came in and exploded as it struck the parapet of the wall under which they sat, bringing it down. Lieutenant James, who was lying wounded on his bed, had a most wonderful escape. A large piece of masonry, weighing upwards of a hundred weight, fell on his bed, breaking it to pieces, and bringing him down on the ground; but he was uninjured. Mr. Lawrence received a severe contusion on the back and head from failing masonry; and this was the extent of the damage. Mrs. Clarke, wife of Lieutenant Clarke of the 21st Native Infantry, died this evening: bad food, privation, confinement, and smells of all kinds, worked their effects.

July 31st – A fine night, and the usual firing. At daylight, the enemy commenced firing heavily on the Church and Residency, from a 24-pounder planted in the neighbourhood of the iron bridge. They also threw in many shells, and fired their guns from the Clock Tower Gate. Our 18-pounders and mortars were employed until 10 a.m. in silencing the enemy's fire. Our sap from the

74   THE DEFENCE OF LUCKNOW

brigade mess made good progress across the road, towards the outhouses occupied by the enemy. Several children have lately died: privation the chief cause. We had received no information whatever since the 26th instant, the date on which we received the only letter we had yet received since the 27th of June. Our reinforcements were due to-day, and their non-arrival led us to suppose that the enemy had succeeded in breaking down the bridge at Bunnee, and arresting the progress of our friends. The flies dreadful, – preventing all rest during the day, and disputing our food with us. The enemy continued to throw in shells all the forenoon, till 2 p.m. when we had a heavy shower: after that, the firing continued as before. In the evening we repaired our defences as far as we could, as, owing to the heavy rain, the earth had settled very considerably. A fine moonlight night, and all quiet, save the usual amount of round shot and musketry.

August 1st – Still no intelligence of any kind, which caused much anxiety, more particularly as some of our supplies for natives were likely to be at an end in twenty days' time. Weather very hot and sultry; small painful boils, covering nearly the whole body, very prevalent. Many deaths among the children, and sickness on the increase. Great inconvenience felt in the hospital for want of space; the sick and wounded sadly crowded, and the building very badly ventilated, as the lower storey was hardly safe from shots. Enemy threw in many shells this morning, and fired unusually sharp with their heavy guns, till about 10 a.m., keeping our guns and mortars fully employed in keeping down their fire. Heat very great; fire gradually slackened off towards noon, but recommenced sharply about 5 p.m. Many round shot, shell, and carcases came in. One of the latter fell into the

The head of the relieving force arriving at the Ballie Gate

76 THE DEFENCE OF LUCKNOW

court-yard of the Begum Kotee, within a few feet of the table at which the staff and commissariat officers were at dinner; but no one was hurt. Several cases of cholera occurred to-day. Efforts made to improve and strengthen our defences during the moonlight nights; but the engineer officers were all sick, and little was done. Our sap in the brigade mess was pushed steadily on, and had attained thirty-eight feet from the shaft this evening.

August 2nd – Fine moonlight night. Sharp firing during some portion of it. Many rockets were thrown in early in the morning. Mr. Hely of the 7th Cavalry died this day of the wound he received on the 20th ult. An artillery sergeant was mortally wounded this morning in the Redan. Enemy fired a salute of some forty guns about 11 a.m. A Seikh sowar of the 3rd Irregular Cavalry deserted to the enemy this morning. The Bhoosa stack fell down to-day, burying ten or twelve bullocks; which, after much labour, were got out. Seven of them were unfortunately dead; thus entailing more labour, as at night we had to bury them: no slight task in such weather, with our jaded and harassed garrison. Towards the evening a heavy cannonade was kept up on both sides. About 5.30 p.m. an eight-inch shell from the enemy struck the Begum Kotee, and, breaking right through the outside wall, exploded in the room in which Lieutenant James of the Commissariat and Mr. Lawrence of the Civil Service were lying on their beds wounded, with one or two servants in the room; providentially all escaped, though the room was set on fire. Heavy firing till midnight.

August 3rd – Smart firing till daylight. Every possible effort was made to strengthen our position and raise the

AUGUST 3–4th 1857

height of our defences. A soldier of the 32nd Foot was shot dead this morning in the centre room of the hospital; showing how little safety anywhere existed against the enemy's fire.

A new loop-hole on the top of the brigade mess, which it was discovered commanded a distant and much frequented lane in the city, was made use of by Lieutenant Sewell, armed with his Enfield rifle; the distance being not above 750 yards, the conical bullets most effectually cleared the lanes of the sepoys, as they lounged up it, and quickened the paces of the citizens as they crossed and recrossed.

Enemy unusually slack in firing after dark till about 10 p.m., when they recommenced firing, and continued it during the night. The engineers continued their endeavours to strengthen our position, by heightening the abattis near the Redan. A fine moonlight night. Several cannon shots were heard in the distance, but no intelligence of any kind reached us.

August 4th – The enemy fired a great number of rounds from their guns at intervals during the night. Musketry fire was slack this morning. No news of any kind. Could get no messengers to go out with a letter, though it was made so small that it went into half a quill; but it had been spread abroad that the enemy would kill any one leaving the garrison, and this deterred any one from endeavouring to carry a letter to our friends, no matter how great the reward might be that was held out.

Many officers and men are laid up with fever and dysentery. Our stored attah was nearly expended, and in a few days' time we should have to commence that which we had ground, which now amounted to about 500 maunds. At 2 p.m. the firing of all kinds was very slack; indeed, for long intervals, not a shot was to be heard. The officers, also, who relieve one another as look-outs on the top of the Residency, reported that a smaller number of men than usual were to be seen on the move. An Eurasian, attached to the party working Dr. Fayrer's guns, was shot dead while working the 18-pounder guns this day, by a man said to be not sixty yards off. Several convalescents have been moved from the hospital to other quarters, and with happy results both as regards themselves and those left in the hospital, which greatly wanted a free circulation of air. Towards dusk many shells came in, and one exploded in the second brigade square; fortunately, it was seen coming, and no harm ensued. The powder magazine was made as secure as possible, by putting heavy beams across the roof, and covering them with two feet of earth. A fine night, but very much firing till midnight.

August 5th – Sent off another letter to the officer commanding the relieving force, of which we could gain no intelligence; though we conjecture the advance of our force had been arrested by the enemy at the bridge of Bunnee. Heavy showers during the day. Musket-proof shutters were completed for the embrasure of the 18-pounders to the left of the hospital. Many of the convalescent patients removed to the Thug Gaol Barracks, which gave them a slight change, and created more room in the hospital. Efforts made to clear some of the drains, and reduce the stench which pervades the garrison. At sunset the enemy were seen at a distance in some force, with drums and fifes playing, marching from the direction of the river towards the Cawnpore road. Soon after, they threw many shells into us, and continued to do so for some time. About 8 p.m. all became tolerably quiet.

August 6th – The enemy fired several shots, from a 24-pounder, at the Residency, one of which unfortunately fractured the arm of Ensign Studdy of the 32nd Foot, as he sat down to breakfast; rendering amputation necessary. This gun caused us great annoyance, from its calibre, and firing so frequently as it did into the Residency. Unfortunately its distance from our position, and its situation in the midst of buildings, rendered it impossible to take it by the bayonet; neither could our gunners see it, so that to shell it was our only resource.

Less firing than usual. The enemy again ascended into the upper story of Johannes's house, and from thence caused much annoyance to the position of the brigade mess, where the cooking went on. They succeeded in killing a sweeper. Terrible heat; Brigadier Inglis suffered from its effects. Various rumours afloat in the garrison; some of which seemed to have originated either with a servant of Mr. Gubbins, or some member of his post. The Residency is at last to be entirely vacated by the officers of the 32nd and others now resident there. Last night was spent in earthing in the magazine, as several shots had lately gone unpleasantly near. A carcase came into the Begum Kotee in the afternoon, into the room in which Lieutenant James (wounded), Mr. Lawrence (wounded), and Ensign Keir (sick), were lying; it set some of the things in the room on fire, but was speedily extinguished without injury to any one. Much bugling, drumming, and firing towards evening. After dark the enemy fired heavily from their guns in front of the Residency. Our engineers and a working party were busy all this night at Innes's house, making a battery for an

80   THE DEFENCE OF LUCKNOW

18-pounder, to be moved down in order to endeavour to
silence a 24-pounder of the enemy's, which had been
doing much mischief by firing through the church and
Residency. About 9 p.m. a sepoy of the 1st Oude
Irregular Infantry, who took out a letter to the officer
commanding the relieving force, came in; he stated that
he had delivered it, and that he had received a letter in
reply which he had lost in coming in to us. Half-an-hour
later, another man, a sepoy of the 48th, who had been
sent into the town two days previously to try and gain
intelligence, returned, and stated he had been confined
several days by the enemy; and he in a great measure
corroborated the statement of the sepoy of the 1st Oude
Irregular Infantry: this loss of the letter was a great
mortification to us, as it might have explained what was
at this time inexplicable – the retirement towards
Cawnpore of General Havelock's force, after apparently
the greatest success on this side of the Ganges.

August 7th – We worked hard at our new battery at
Innes's house, and got it ready; an 18-pounder was taken
down and in position by daylight, whence it commenced
firing, and soon silenced the enemy's guns. The enemy,
however, fired heavily from some others, and about
8 a.m. a shell burst close to the Residency and mortally
wounded two of the best men in the 32nd, the one a
colour-sergeant and the other an orderly-room clerk.
Captain Waterman of the 13th was wounded through the
hand by a musket ball at Innes's post this morning.
Several cases of cholera. Every effort made to increase
the number of men to grind wheat for the force. Exceedingly heavy rain during the middle of the day.

The hose into our mine near Johannes's house got
damped, and required all the tamping to be removed.

Our position greatly flooded, which rendered it most wretched for those who had to be in trenches night and day. The artillery canteen closed, in consequence of the gross irregularities which prevailed, and its contents removed to the canteen of the 32nd Regiment, from which the artillery were in future supplied. The heavy rain seemed to make the stench which pervaded the place worse, and this evening it was fearful. Several cases of cholera occurred to-day. The enemy's cannon knocked down a portion of the verandah of the Residency, also the verandah of Delprat's house at the Cawnpore battery: a few shells came in in the evening.

August 8th – A tolerably quiet night. Dr. McDonnell, of the 41st Native Infantry, died early this morning of cholera. A soldier of the 32nd was shot, and a native woman-servant of Mrs. Banks had her thigh broken by musketry at Mr. Gubbins's post this forenoon.

A heavy smoke was distinctly seen in the far distance in the direction of the Cawnpore road. Many reports were made of heavy firing being heard in the same direction: a Sikh attached to the cavalry brought repeated accounts of it, but no European, save Captains Forbes and Hawes, of Mr. Gubbins's post, could say he heard it. The natives (some of them) very anxious about the arrival of the reinforcements, of whom we could hear nothing.

In the afternoon, a regiment of infantry, about 600 strong, with drums beating, marching in quarter distance column with colours, was seen marching through the city, in the direction of the Cawnpore road.

Seven hundred yards from the brigade-mess was a street in the city which was commanded by Lieutenant Sewell's double Enfield rifle, and on which spot he had killed several sepoys and others: this was this afternoon barricaded right across, which was a nuisance, as it entirely obstructed our view of what passed along. Lieutenant Bryce of the artillery, who had been severely wounded, died of cholera.

No intelligence came in this evening, and much anxiety as to our reinforcements was evinced by some of our native troops and servants. Rice was served out to most of the natives in lieu of flour, and wheat to the native camp-followers, in order to husband our stock of flour. All the tea and coffee for the Europeans expended; the last issue being made yesterday. This was the first day on which we had no casualty.

August 9th – The heat excessive, and children sunk rapidly under the effects of want of good air, food and exercise: several deaths occurred among them, both yesterday and to-day. The enemy fired heavily in the morning, but providentially no one was hurt. Ensign Studdy, who had had his arm amputated from the effects of a 24-pounder shot, died this morning. The enemy were thought to have recommenced mining near the Redan battery.

Divine service was performed in the brigade mess-house to all officers not on duty. No signs or symptoms of our reinforcements. In the middle of the day Ensign Loughnan of the 13th (on duty at Innes's house) went out with a few men and quietly spiked a small gun of the enemy's, and returned without any loss. A very heavy shower in the evening, which filled our trenches. One or two doolies were seen going across the Goomtee, accompanied by sepoys. About 9 p.m. a Seikh sowar of the 3rd Oude Irregular Cavalry came in by the Seikh battery. His having been permitted to pass the enemy's outposts induced a belief that he had come in to try and make

AUGUST 9–10th 1857

the other Seikhs desert; consequently he was placed under British bayonets, and not allowed to converse with any one.

August 10th – About 10 a.m. a great number of sepoys, probably 1600, were seen, with two guns, marching up our left flank and across the Cawnpore road, behind their trenches. Very shortly after, a large force was seen to be approaching the bridge of boats from cantonments; and, in consequence, all were quickly at their posts. About half an hour after, the enemy fired a shell into the Begum Kotee, which appeared to be a signal; for the instant after, a mine was sprung opposite to Johannes's house, which blew in a great portion of the house occupied by Mr. Schilling and the Martiniere boys, and entirely destroyed our pallisades and defences for the space of sixty feet. One of the heaviest timbers was pitched right on the top of the brigade mess-house, among the officers and men of the 32nd, who occupied the post. As soon as the smoke blew away, the enemy pushed up, under a tremendous musketry fire, right into Johannes's house and garden, and into all the buildings close round the Cawnpore battery; but all their efforts to enter our position were met with such a steady fire, that they fell back, and kept up an incessant fire of musketry on our defences. About thirty of them, however, lodged themselves in the ditch of the Cawnpore battery, within a few feet of our guns. A hand grenade was rolled over right into the centre of them, on which they bolted and ran back, exposed to a sharp fusillade from our people on the top of the brigade-mess.

While this was going on, a very sharp attack was made on Mrs. Sago's house, where the enemy blew up a mine, which destroyed some of the outhouses and blew two

84 THE DEFENCE OF LUCKNOW

soldiers out into the road, outside our defences: extra-ordinary to relate, they fell unhurt, and got safely back to their posts. The enemy then made their attack, but were soon driven back with considerable loss, and confined themselves to keeping up a tremendous storm of round shot and musketry on our position, which after two hours, in a great measure, subsided. About 5 p.m., they made a sudden rush on Captain Saunders's post. One of the enemy even seized a bayonet of one of the 84th Foot, and tried to wrench it off through a loophole, but was instantly shot; after a smart fusillade, which lasted for about 25 minutes, they withdrew, and gradually the fire ceased.

About 9 p.m. a third attack was made, and was similarly repulsed; nor were these efforts confined to the places above noted. At Innes's house, Anderson's, and Mr. Gubbins's post, large bodies of men came forward, bringing up large scaling-ladders, several of which they abandoned. During the day, we lost three Europeans and two sepoys killed, and about twice that number wounded. Our garrison were under arms the entire day, the heat was excessive, and all were greatly exhausted; nevertheless, every officer and man remained under arms all night: after 10 o'clock all became tolerably quiet. Captain Power, of the 32nd, who had been wounded early in the siege, died in hospital to-day, and Major Anderson, chief engineer, was reported very dangerously ill. The enemy must have had a considerable loss this day, as a great number of them were seen to fall; and we threw 150 shells, besides great quantities of round shot and grape, from which also many casualties must have occurred.

August 11th – A slight alarm about 2 a.m., after which all subsided into the usual routine firing. A very

Highlanders at Lucknow

86   THE DEFENCE OF LUCKNOW

fine morning; very little to be seen of the enemy, who however were not idle, as they were to-day busily employed constructing earthworks and trenches in various directions close to our position. Early in the morning the enemy fired many round shot, some of which struck the Residency, already much shattered; and about noon a very distressing accident took place. There was a high wind, and it brought down a great portion of the left wing, on the ground floor of which, in a room, six men of the 32nd were asleep. They were completely buried in the ruins. Two were got out alive after very great exertions, but the remaining four were left under the ruins. Immediate arrangements made for the removal of the few European women and children who still occupied one of the rooms on the ground floor.

Major Anderson, chief engineer, died during the afternoon. He had been ailing before the siege, but on the commencement rallied somewhat, owing to the excitement and novelty of the position. Latterly he fell off again, and to-day expired; his death no doubt hastened by the impossibility of any change of air or diet. The lookout officers yesterday reported having seen some few doolies going across the river with sepoys after the day of attack, and to-day some dead and wounded were also seen being conveyed away. The enemy were busy close under Mr. Gubbins's ramparts, whence they had once before been expelled by some hand grenades. At the corner of the Seikh square also, from across the road, they amused themselves by pushing out over the wall bamboos with lighted straw at the end; but with what object was not very clear: in the meanwhile not one of them showed themselves, but kept well under cover. Smart firing in the evening. The corpse of a soldier of the

AUGUST 11–12th 1857

32nd was extricated from the ruins of the Residency; three others still remained.

August. 12th – A fine moonlight night. About 3.30 a.m. the enemy suddenly commenced a very heavy fire of round shot and musketry, which lasted for three-quarters of an hour. We kept close, and hardly fired a shot, beyond throwing a few shells. At day light, they commenced a very heavy cannonade and musketry fire on the Cawnpore battery; this gradually became so sharp, that it was impossible to work our guns, or even remain in the battery; and we were obliged to withdraw every one but the sentry, as the enemy's round shot had destroyed our musketry shutters, and completely swept the battery: later in the day, our sentry, the only man in the battery, was killed by a round shot. This portion of our position caused us great anxiety, as we were quite unable to hold it as it should be held; we would not withdraw our guns, for fear of giving the enemy confidence. The enemy were busily employed to-day also in digging close to Sago's house. In order to see what they were about, at 12 o'clock a sortie was made with twelve Europeans of the 32nd Foot under Lieutenant Chlery, accompanied by Lieutenant Hutchinson of the Engineers. The enemy were, however, well on the alert, and had a large covering party over their work, and as our men appeared, they threw in such a heavy fire that our people were compelled to retire; this brought on a very great fire from all that side of the enemy's attack, and they kept up a smart fire of round shot and musketry for fully an hour, when it gradually subsided. Finding we were unequal to meet the enemy by a sortie, we determined to push on our mine as fast as possible, and continue working all day and night, hoping to blow them up.

In the evening we had as strong working parties of Europeans as we could afford, and removed from the Cawnpore battery, a 9-pounder which had been disabled by a round shot of the enemy. We also dug a trench and threw up earth on the top of our parapets, and endeavoured to our utmost to repair the damage the enemy had done, and make the place as strong as possible. Several shells came in after dusk. The heat throughout the day was excessive, and there were several fatal cases of cholera, and also several deaths among the children, who were all greatly emaciated.

In the evening, a letter to General Havelock, rolled up and put inside a quill, was despatched by the hands of an old woman; she left our position about 9 p.m., and we hoped, would be permitted to pass the enemy's sentries without being stopped. During the past forty-five days, we had sent by different hands, in a similar manner, some twenty letters, to only one of which was any reply received. The garrison, very greatly harassed and fatigued from continued exertion night and day and want of rest.

August 13th – An excessively hot night. During the early part of the morning the enemy threw in a very heavy fire, which lasted for nearly half an hour, when all subsided into the usual routine firing.

Our mine near Sago's house was pushed on all night with the greatest possible speed. Every possible means was adopted by the enemy to prevent our miners working, and as only a wall and a few feet of ground divided the two parties, they resorted to squibs, rockets, brickbats, and lights at the end of bamboos, to annoy our workmen. As the latter were thrust forward with the hope of setting fire to our tiled outhouses, the ends were successively cut off by us. Several reports alive in the

AUGUST 13th 1857

garrison, but on what grounds, or how stated, no one could say. However, as these were all more or less favourable to us, and encouraging to the natives, if credited, no harm was done.

Shortly before 10 a.m. the engineers reported our countermine as ready; the neighbouring outposts and garrisons were duly warned, and the mine fired, with the happiest results: the brick house in which the enemy was, and from which they had started their mine, settled down, burying all inside; the earth was thrown up to a considerable height, and only one outhouse of our own, of no consequence, destroyed. Up to the last moment, the people inside the enemy's mine were hard at work, and after the explosion the groans of the sufferers were plainly audible. In the course of the day, some few of the enemy were shot from Sago's post. In the afternoon, after several shells had been thrown in to drive as many out as possible, it was determined to go out and see what the enemy were doing near Mr. Gubbins's post. A hole being cut in the wall out of our defences, a party of Europeans, with the engineer officers, went out and found a deep trench dug through the outhouses for some distance towards our position. The work was not deemed of any great importance, and after it had been well examined, the party withdrew.

Many cases of fever to-day, and four deaths in hospital among the Europeans. Enemy very quiet during the evening; unusually so, till about 10 p.m., when they threw an 8-inch shell into our position. This appeared to be a signal; for instantly they commenced a tremendous fire with round shot and musketry, which lasted half an hour, and completely lit up the darkness around. They were busy mining us in several places, and their work-men could be distinctly heard at work. Our engineers

90   THE DEFENCE OF LUCKNOW

were hard at work, trying with the best means at their disposal to frustrate their efforts; but our people were so harassed that they were not capable of any prolonged exertion. A shaft, however, for a mine was made in Mr. Anderson's house, and sunk to the extent of eight feet, in view to running a sap to meet the enemy. Heat very great, and mosquitoes, bugs, and fleas most troublesome.

August 14th – Enemy unusually quiet all the morning; more so than they had yet been. Our people were all busy preparing new sandbags, as the old ones were so rotten, from long exposure to the rain, that they would bear no removal: also in countermining the enemy from out of a corner of Anderson's house. A Mater came in this morning, but could give no information. Provision for the cattle growing short; and every means adopted to reduce the daily consumption. The various look-outs reported no movement of the enemy: in a word, it was the quietest day we had yet had. About 4 p.m. they began a more brisk fire. Many cases of fever and several deaths amongst the children. Many rumours abroad regarding our relieving force; but all was conjecture. Most of our outpost houses were now so riddled with round shot, that it was a wonder how any of them stood up at all: indeed most of them were in ruins, and at Mr. Anderson's house part of the garrison had been twice pulled out of the ruins which had suddenly fallen on them; nevertheless, these posts, in spite of many casualties, were held with the same courage and devotion as was displayed the first day of the siege. At dusk we had a severe thunderstorm, with exceedingly heavy rain, which lasted for several hours, falling in a complete deluge; the night was exceedingly dark, with extremely vivid lightning. Lieutenants

AUGUST 14–16th 1857

Fulton and Hutchinson of the Engineers went down and examined all the outhouses in Dr. Fayrer's premises, to see if any mining operations could be heard. They afterwards went down to the Buxee Khana, and examined the wall in front to some distance.

August 15th – Heavy rain till about 3 a.m., when it cleared away, and the morning was beautifully clear and fine. The enemy fired salvos of two and three 18-pounders at once into the Cawnpore battery, and brought down all the outer wall of the house alongside it, which we used as a guardroom; making the place so hot we were obliged to retire our men from it during the heaviest part of the cannonade. Lieutenant Bonham received a severe contusion, from bricks knocked out on him by an 18-pound shot; and later in the day the sentry left in the front part of the battery was killed by a round shot. Lieutenant James Alexander was shot through the arm while laying an 18-pounder in the Hospital battery. Several servants and six bheesties of the 32nd deserted last night. At night, advantage taken of the dark to repair as much as possible the damage done to-day to the Cawnpore battery. About 9 p.m. a pensioner named Ungud, who had been sent out with a letter, returned, bringing a letter from Cawnpore. This was the first night since the siege began that no burial took place.

August 16th – Great progress made in our mine out of Lieutenant Anderson's house, which had now reached a distance of twenty-five feet from the shaft. Also much done in the way of making the Cawnpore battery more secure. Brigadier Inglis slept in it himself. In the early morning the enemy fired a great many round shot, and brought a new gun into position, to play on the corner of

92 THE DEFENCE OF LUCKNOW

the brigade mess-house; also one which fired on Mr. Gubbins's post, but which was soon silenced by a 9-pounder placed in position against it. Divine service performed in the brigade-mess to a few officers who were off duty, and to the ladies. Much round shot fired during the day, but fewer sepoys in sight than usual. Every possible effort was made to curtail the expenditure of our provisions, and make them last as long as possible. The enemy threw in three 8-inch shells during the evening, and fired several round shot during the night.

August 17th – The remaining portion of the Residency was deemed unsafe by the engineers, from the number of round shot that had come through it; and arrangements were made to remove the Europeans. The heat extreme, a heavy cannonade from daylight till 9 a.m., when it gradually slackened. A few round shot were fired through the Residency during the morning. Much progress was made in the mine out of Lieutenant Anderson's house, and a new shaft sunk in the Martiniere School, in view to running a sap towards Johannes's house. The Seikhs mined well, and the payment in cash of two rupees per man for each night's work made the work popular. Between 4 and 5 p.m. the enemy recommenced a slight cannonade, doubtless stirred up by some shells which were thrown during the afternoon. Towards dusk the enemy threw in several shells, and at midnight an 8-inch, which nearly hit our laboratory.

August 18th – At daylight the enemy exploded a large mine under one of our principal posts in the outer square, occupied by the Seikhs; the three officers and three sentries on the top of the house, were blown up into the air and fell among the débris. The guard below were all, however, buried in the ruins, and lost their lives: they were two bandsmen of the 41st, two of the 13th, and a sepoy of the 48th Native Infantry. The officers, though much stunned, on recovering themselves ran away, and all three escaped unhurt. When the smoke had blown away, we discovered that a clear breach had been made into our defences, to the extent of thirty feet in breadth. One of the enemy's leaders sprung on the top of the breach, brandishing his sword and calling on others to follow; but he fell dead instantly from the flank fire of the officers on the top of the brigade-mess. Another instantly followed and shared the same fate, when the rest of the force declined making a home rush. On the first springing of the mine, our garrison was at once under arms, and the reserve of the 84th Foot (eighteen men) were immediately sent down and placed in a position which commanded the breach from the right; while boxes, doors, planks, tents, &c., were rapidly carried down to make as much cover as possible to protect our men against musketry: also a house was pulled down and a road made for a gun; and, after incredible exertions, a 9-pounder was got into a position which commanded all the breach, and was loaded with a double charge of grape. The enemy, by means of some barricaded lanes, contrived to creep up and get possession of the right flank wall of the Seikh square; but our mortar and a 24-pounder howitzer drove the main body off, and a sudden rush at noon cleared away the rest. We re-occupied all the ground we had lost in the morning, and also took possession of the houses previously held by the enemy, and which were situated between the Seikh square and Mr. Gubbins's house. No time was lost in destroying them, and by sunset 400lbs. of gunpowder had cleared away many of the houses from which the enemy had

94 THE DEFENCE OF LUCKNOW

most annoyed us. By this time the breach was securely barricaded against any sudden rush, and at night a working party completed it. In addition to the eight men lost in the explosion, we had this day one of the 32nd killed, and a volunteer (M. De Prât) and three of the 32nd wounded. Nothing could exceed the zeal with which *all* the natives worked to secure the breach, and make a road for a gun. The heat was fearful, and this was one of the most harassing days we had, all ranks being hard at work from daylight till dark, under a dreadful sun. Lieutenant Fletcher, 48th Regiment Native Infantry, on look-out duty at the top of the Residency, was shot through the arm, and had his telescope shivered by a rifle-ball, while reconnoitring. Lieutenant Graham was also hit on the chest with a spent ball. For further accounts of the explosion of the mine, see the report of the disaster by an eye-witness, marked (II.) in the Appendix.

August 19th – The enemy rather lively with their large guns this morning. Firing more particularly at the guard-rooms on the top of the brigade-mess, which were by this time well-riddled. About 2 p.m. the engineers, Messrs. Fulton, Hutchinson, and Anderson, with a small party, went out on the premises which we yesterday seized, for the purpose of blowing up some more houses and buildings. This party was supported by some Europeans and Seikhs, kept inside the square. The enemy showed nowhere, and save for a few dropping shots, their presence would not have been known.

It is worthy of notice, that even through the Pucka buildings, the enemy dug communicating trenches, probably to escape the effects of our shells; which, however, they had not always been successful in doing, as several pools of blood showed us. In the afternoon we experienced a smart cannonade, and about dusk had a heavy shower which stayed it for a while, and after 8 p.m. it subsided nearly entirely into a musketry fire.

August 20th – A heavy fire of musketry towards daylight, when the enemy began the heaviest cannonade we had yet had; particularly on the Cawnpore battery, in front of which they had put another gun in position. For three hours they fired continually, and a great portion of Mons. De Prât's house fell in. Their round shot came in through the Thug Jail, and enfiladed it; fortunately it struck high, and no casualty occurred: they also threw some shrapnel, as yesterday. Our guard rooms on the top of the brigade mess were now entirely demolished by round shot, which came through them almost unceasingly. An 8-inch shell went into the Residency, and exploded on the staircase. A soldier of the 32nd Foot was killed in the 18-pounder battery, at Dr. Fayrer's, by a musket-ball which struck him in the head. We were busy all night at our mine, which was now completed, and we hope to be able to load it and have it ready to fire by daylight to-morrow morning. Many men were seen in the early part of the day, moving about in the bazaar (most of them sepoys). It was difficult to say what they were about, as they were moving both ways. Lieutenant Cunliffe of the artillery was slightly wounded this morning in the knee by a musket ball. Great mortality amongst the children in the garrison, and a great deal of sickness prevailed, particularly fever. All the tea and sugar for the Europeans had been for some time expended, save a small supply which had been reserved for the use of the sick and wounded. The enemy again commenced to undermine the lane running from the Cawnpore battery

Street in Lucknow

behind the brigade-mess, and were also engaged in some other work to the right of Johannes's house. Much firing during the evening. Captain Lowe of the 32nd Foot, had a very narrow escape; an eight-inch shell burst close to him in the trenches, and slightly wounded him in the hand, and cut off the arm of a soldier alongside him. The enemy made an attempt to burn down the gates at the Baillie Guard, by eluding the vigilance of the sentries and piling up logs of wood and combustibles outside the gate. It burnt fiercely, but was soon extinguished by the water-carriers of the 13th, without damage to the gates: the fire was the signal for a heavy fusillade, which lasted nearly half an hour.

August 21st – At daybreak all was prepared and ready for the blowing-up of our mine, and the simultaneous sortie of fifty Europeans under Captain M'Cabe and Lieutenant Browne (divided into two parties), for the purpose of spiking the enemy's guns which fired into the mess house, and in order to hold Johannes's house while the engineer officers blew it up. Precisely at 5 p.m. the mine, containing 400 lbs. of powder, was sprung, and as soon as the dust and smoke had in a measure subsided, the party ran out, drove the enemy (who were taken by surprise, and made but a slight show of resistance) from their guns (two), and spiked them both, and retained possession of Johannes's house, while the engineers made arrangements for blowing it up. These were soon completed, and the party withdrawn. A slow match was applied, and the house laid in ruins. Our losses were one of the 84th killed, one sergeant (84th) mortally wounded, one of the 32nd dangerously wounded, one slightly wounded, and a sergeant of the artillery killed. The operation was entirely successful, and rid us of a house from which the enemy had, from the commencement of the siege, annoyed us greatly. Captain Barlow, of the 50th Native Infantry, died somewhat suddenly in hospital this morning. The grass and jungle all round had grown to a very great height, and would have given cover to a number of men to approach close up to our position unobserved. In the afternoon, a boy about twelve years of age was seen close to the Baillie Guard gate, picking up bullets that had been fired. A sepoy of the 13th on sentry-duty saw him, covered him with his musket, and compelled him to come in. An eight-inch shell fell on the top of the Residency about 9 p.m., and exploded, fortunately without injuring any one.

August 22nd – Mrs. Green, of the 48th Native Infantry, died early this morning. There had been also

98 THE DEFENCE OF LUCKNOW

many deaths among children during the few previous days. Many of our supplies were entirely expended, and the garrison were put to great inconvenience for the want of tobacco, of which for some time past there had been none to issue. Still more stringent measures adopted to prevent the consumption of flour; and wheat was issued to all non-combatants who had time to grind it. A fine clear night, with less musketry and more cannon firing than usual. Many of our defences were greatly injured from the late heavy rain and the incessant cannonade of the enemy. Last night repairs were made to the Cawnpore and Redan batteries, both of which still required much to be done to them. To-day an European sentry inside the Baillie Guard gate, was shot dead by a rifleman: the ball went through some sand bags put up for his protection. A sepoy of the 13th was also hit in the knee this morning from the same loop-hole. Arrangements were made to knock the place down to-morrow morning at daylight with a 24-pounder howitzer. Sergeant Ryder, of the artillery, was killed dead by a musket ball to-day in the churchyard. Up to this date, we had lost since the siege commenced on the 30th of June, by killed, wounded, and sickness: 101 men of the 32nd Foot, not including officers; and of the detachment of the 84th, consisting originally of fifty men, eleven had been killed and died of wounds and disease since the above date. Reports of distant firing being heard, vague rumours were afloat; but these excited little attention *now,* so often had they been in circulation, giving rise to false hopes of our reinforcements being near.

Captain Hawes, of the 63rd Native Infantry, was wounded this afternoon by a musket ball through the side and arm, while on the look-out from the top of the defences at Mr. Gubbins's post. After dark we had two

AUGUST 22–23rd 1857

eight-inch shells and several shrapnell sent in. One of the former carried off the leg of a native (who died soon after), and slightly wounded another. Repairs continued in the Cawnpore and Redan batteries. The want of tea and sugar much felt, and very large prices offered for stores of any kind.

August 23rd – A heavy cannonade from the enemy, from daylight till about 10 p.m., when it slackened. Their principal efforts were against the brigade-mess house and Cawnpore battery; the former they seriously damaged, and succeeded in entirely levelling the guard-houses on the top; both of which had fallen in, and there was no longer any cover for our musketry to fire from. Our ranks were rapidly thinning. Two men were again this morning mortally wounded by musketry fire. The enemy were busily employed in digging on all sides, more particularly in front of the Redan; but it was very difficult to say what their object was, as they dug deep trenches in all directions. Continued reports of distant firing being heard. The enemy fired heavily from their guns in the afternoon, and did considerable damage to our defences. A working party employed after dark, making a magazine for the powder and shells lodged in the Post-office.

We had work nightly for at least 300 men; as we had the defences to repair daily, supplies to remove from godowns which were fallen in from the effects of the enemy's shot, mines to countermine, guns to remove, barricades to erect, corpses to bury, and rations to serve out; but with our weak, harassed, and daily diminishing garrison, we could seldom produce as working parties more than three fatigue parties of eight or ten men each relief; and the Europeans were capable of but little

100   THE DEFENCE OF LUCKNOW

exertion, as from want of sleep, hard work night and day, and constant exposure, their bodily strength was greatly diminished. The enemy threw in an 8-inch shell about 9 p.m. and fired all the evening. Divine service was performed at the brigade-mess in the morning, and in the afternoon, at Dr. Fayrer's; the sacrament was administered on both occasions.

August 24th – This morning, at about 2 o'clock, the enemy opened a very heavy fire, both of round shot and musketry; commencing and concluding the same apparently on the signal of a fireball thrown up on each occasion. The Judicial Garrison house, under command of Captain Germon, being in a most dangerous state from the effects of round shot, all the women and wounded men, also children, were removed from that post, as well as from all the other outposts in that quarter, into the Begum Kotee in the neighbourhood. A sergeant of the 84th was dangerously wounded coming up from Mrs. Sago's house, by a sharpshooter. Lieutenant Bonham, of the artillery, was busily employed perfecting his arrangements for using an 8-inch mortar as a howitzer. The experiment succeeded very well yesterday evening.

The verandah of the Residency on the west side came entirely down this morning. The commissariat stores in the godown underneath were removed in the evening, as some of the arches of the lower story were cracked, and a heavy cannonade would have brought the whole place down. Arrangements were made this day for still further reducing the rations of Europeans. A kitmutghar came in from the city last night: his account was so suspicious, that he was placed under an European guard, as he might have tampered with the natives. To-day we threw two shells a long way into the city, in the direction of the palace. The enemy tolerably quiet; towards the middle of the day confining themselves to sharpshooting at every one they saw move about in our position. Mr. MacRae of the Civil Engineer Department was very badly hit in the shoulder this afternoon, while assisting in laying a mortar in the Post-office; and a sergeant and a private were badly wounded early in the day, while going to their post. The enemy possessed many excellent rifle shots, and fired out of their loopholes from the houses around with great certainty; occasioning us a daily loss of from three to five men. Two sepoys of the 13th were also slightly wounded by random shots before daybreak this morning. Several shells came in this evening; and about 12 p.m. the enemy opened a tremendous fire on all sides, of round shot, grape, and musketry, which lasted for an hour: the fire was very heavy, but they made no effort to storm, though their bugles sounded the advance repeatedly.

August 25th – There was the usual heavy cannonade this morning from the enemy, which continued from 5 to 9 a.m., when it slackened. All the remaining porter in store (thirty-nine casks) was got out of the Residency, and removed to another place, consequent on the unsafe state of the building; nearly one half of which had fallen from round shot, and the remaining portion was likely to follow. The magazine for the Post-office battery completed. In the night two sepoys of the 11th were slightly wounded by random shots. Several coolies were seen coming through the bazaar from the direction of the Cawnpore road. Sharpshooting all day long from the enemy, who had also got a new gun in position to the right of Mr. Gubbins's post. One mine completed, and three others steadily progressing; the enemy digging on all sides.

102 THE DEFENCE OF LUCKNOW

August 26th – The enemy commenced the day with a very heavy fire of round shot and musketry a little before daylight, which subsided in a great measure in about half an hour. Their earthworks had been added to during the night; but it was difficult to distinguish new work, as the whole of our position was now surrounded with them on every side quite close up to us. A jemadar of the 71st was shot dead near the Redan this morning by one of the enemy's riflemen. The house of Innes was reported to be in a dangerous state, in consequence of the repeated round shots through it. Also reports were made of the enemy mining at the Redan. The enemy unusually quiet, and very little firing went on during the middle of the day, but they were busily employed in making trenches round us in every direction, and worked particularly hard in front of the Redan, with many coolies. No intelligence whatever. One or two servants deserted last night, and there were reports that all the servants were thinking of leaving us, unless our reinforcements arrived soon.

August 27th – A good deal of rain during the night. A heavy cannonade from the enemy, and the usual amount of musketry fire all the morning.

To-day, the supplies of the late Brigadier-General Sir Henry Lawrence, K.C.B., were sold by auction. The brandy realised from 140 to 160 rupees (16*l.*) per dozen; beer averaged from 60 to 70 rupees (7*l.*); sherry 70 rupees; hermetically sealed hams from 70 to 75 rupees (7*l.* 10*s.*) each; a bottle of honey 45 rupees (4*l.* 10*s.*); rifle gunpowder, 16 rupees per lb. (1*l.* 12*s.*); small cakes of chocolate, from 30 to 40 rupees (3*l.* to 4*l.*); and other things in proportion. Sugar (had there been any for sale) would have commanded almost any price.

AUGUST 27–28th 1857

The enemy brought another gun into position opposite the racket court, and where we had no means of replying to them. A soldier of the 32nd was very seriously wounded this morning by a musket-ball, while sitting in the verandah of Dr. Fayrer's house. In the evening a 3-pounder shot killed a soldier of the 32nd and carried away the arm of another. A native officer of the 13th was wounded through the foot by a musket-ball. Our miners (working in the gallery we had run out thirty-three feet to the right of the brigade mess-house) heard the enemy distinctly mining towards us. Their sap seemed to run for the centre of the brigade mess.

August 28th – Heavy rain nearly all night, which considerably injured our sap to the right of the brigade mess, in consequence of it leaking; the rain ceasing at daylight, we set to work, and in a few hours got it cleared out, and had our people at work again. A good deal of fever prevalent, and great mortality among the children, who faded away rapidly from want of proper food. A smart cannonade at daylight from the enemy, who fired heavily with two guns on Mr. Gubbins's house; fortunately no casualties occurred. Last night, three men deserted to the enemy from Mr. Gubbins's post. One, a chuprassee of Mr. G.'s, took with him 400 rupees (40l.) belonging to different people; four servants belonging to officers also deserted.

Lieutenant Bonham fired his mortar, equipped as a howitzer, fourteen times during the day, against the new battery erected against Mr. Gubbins's post, and with considerable success, having struck it ten times; but their battery was of great strength, and required a good deal more battering to do it much mischief. We waited with impatience for the enemy's miners to break through

104   THE DEFENCE OF LUCKNOW

our gallery, and were obliged to stop our own men, as the enemy left off work immediately they heard our people's pickaxe.

This night we learnt, by a letter from General Havelock, dated Cawnpore, the 24th instant, that we had no hope of being relieved for another twenty-five days.

August 29th – Cooler weather. Our miners busily employed endeavouring to break into the enemy's gallery, which, though quite close to our own, had not yet been found. The magazine sergeants at work, making an expence magazine in the Begum Kotee. The upper story of Mr. Gubbins's house was no longer safe, owing to the numbers of round shot through it, and the ladies were re-moved. Much difficulty was experienced in finding quarters for them, every place being so crowded, and the ladies were already four and five together in very small badly ventilated native buildings; dreadful smells pervading the whole place, from the half-buried bodies of men, horses, and bullocks, and also from the drains – some of which were fearfully offensive, as we had no means of attending to them. Several more servants deserted last night; which caused the very greatest inconvenience, as already very few officers had any. About 10 a.m. our miners broke into the enemy's gallery, which they immediately abandoned, and began to fill in the shaft; we as instantly applied a barrel of powder at the farther end of their sap, and blew up their work altogether. Our men brought away their lantern, tools, and a bottle of oil, which in their haste they had left. Very heavy rain all the forenoon.

Sickness became daily more prevalent, and a number of officers and 'the uncovenanted' were daily placed on the sick list. To-day it was decided to issue one month's

The King's Palace

pay after the 1st proximo, for the month of July. The heavy rain caused one of the enemy's mines, running towards the outpost called Mrs. Sago's house, to fall in. This mine was never known to us, or even suspected. Many and grave doubts and suspicions were entertained that the enemy were running a mine towards the Redan battery. Lieutenant Fulton, Garrison Engineer, did not, however, share in this opinion. A native artilleryman, who belonged to a number entertained by Mr. Gubbins, deserted from his post while on sentry over one of the guns in Mr. G.'s compound. A European sentry fired at him, but did not succeed in hitting him.

Now that it appeared evident that the siege must last in all probability another month, increased care and vigilance in the issuing of all stores was observed. The rain cleared off towards evening. A considerable cannonade all through the night.

*

August 30th – A heavy cannonade all night. Four half-castes (Christians) one of whom had been made a local sergeant, and was head-writer in Captain Weston's office, deserted to the enemy; having broke open the door in the barrier they had to defend, and left the post unprotected. He took with him, in addition to Captain Boileau's gun, five drummers, formerly in the king of Oude's service, two drummers of the 48th, and some ten native servants. An eight-inch shell burst in the native hospital this morning, killing one native and wounding two others. An attack was expected to-day, and everything was prepared as far as possible to repel it. A good many cases of fever. Divine service was performed at the brigade mess at noon, and at Mr. Gubbins's house at 2 p.m., when the sacrament was administered, and at Dr. Fayrer's house at half-past 5 p.m. To-day, Lieut. Bonham, of the artillery, was very severely wounded by a musket-ball, while sitting in the doorway of the Post-office: he was a very great loss to the garrison, having very greatly distinguished himself throughout the siege; particularly in the accuracy with which he used his mortars, and the excellent practice he had made with a mortar which he had made to act as a howitzer. This was the third time he had been wounded since hostilities began on the 30th of June. Very little firing during the middle of the day, and not much movement observable among the enemy. A European soldier of the 32nd died very suddenly to-day; he lost the use of his side from sleeping in the wet trenches, and died in hospital a few hours after. Europeans and natives all greatly distressed on account of the want of tobacco, of which we have had none left for distribution for a considerable time past. Great difficulty was experienced in getting shelter for women and children; so many houses had been destroyed

AUGUST 30–31st 1857

by the round shot and shells of the enemy: all suffered greatly from being crowded together in low, small, badly ventilated buildings. The dreadful stench which pervaded that part of the defences held by the commissariat officers and the uncovenanted service, exceeded all belief. It arose from the decayed entrails of the bullocks and sheep daily killed by the butchers, and of which we had no means of disposing, but by throwing them over the defences: the decayed boosah and vegetable matter which here also abounded, assisting in creating a stench which was probably never exceeded. Nearly every officer who slept at this post was laid up with fever at one time or another; but as it was one of the weakest parts of our defences, it was absolutely requisite that two officers should be ever with the party occupying it. A false alarm at sunset, and a heavy cannonade brought the day's proceedings to a close.

August 31st – The enemy fired at intervals very hard, both guns and musketry, particularly towards daylight. Then we found they had got another very large gun, apparently a 32-pounder, in position under the Lutkun Durwaza, and about 100 yards from the Baillie Guard gates, on which it fired several times, smashing two ammunition waggons with which the gates were barricaded. Towards the middle of the day the enemy were unusually quiet, confining themselves to sharpshooting. An excellent artillery sergeant was killed at Mr. Gubbins's post, by a rifle-ball, which struck him in the side.

The heat excessive. In the evening, the kitmutghar of the late Captain Hayes, military secretary, who had come in some ten days before, and was believed to be a spy, escaped from the 84th Guard during the night, and

108   THE DEFENCE OF LUCKNOW

contrived to get clear away. He had been kept in confinement from the time of his coming in, and had not been allowed to converse with any one; and therefore could give little or no information. About 10 p.m. the enemy very suddenly opened from nearly all their guns, and threw in a heavy fire of musketry, which subsided in about half an hour. All the 13th Native Infantry employed in making a new sunken battery to the right of the guard-room, in order to oppose the battery of the enemy which was located in the Lutkun Durwaza. Our people in the Redan battery had a narrow escape from an 8-inch shell, which just cleared the parapet and exploded outside.

September 1st – A fine breezy morning. Not very much firing; but a great deal of bugling was heard among the enemy's troops during the early part of the morning. Rumours that the half-caste Christians who deserted had been murdered. The enemy's 24-pounder fired several shots during the morning, which took effect on the gates, smashing them considerably. The enemy reported to be running another mine towards the brigade mess.

Our third sap from Anderson's post nearly completed, and considerable progress made in the one commenced out of Sago's house. All the boys in garrison above ten years of age were collected and set to work with handmills, to assist in grinding flour for the use of the garrison. Sickness showed itself amongst the bullocks; and in the last two days two bullocks had to be suddenly killed, in order to save the meat. This was most unfortunate, as the stock in hand would not last (even at the reduced rate of rations) the time we might probably be besieged. Arrangements were made to have some

SEPTEMBER 1–2nd 1857

artillery and irregular cavalry horses that were
wounded, or from want of condition were unserviceable,
turned out on this evening. The last cook-boy of the
artillery absconded last night. This put the men to much
inconvenience, as they had now to draw their rations
with Her Majesty's 32nd Regiment; but it was better for
the service, as now there was no excuse for any of the
guns' crews leaving their batteries for their food. This
morning some fresh beef was accidentally removed from
the slaughter-yard in one of the magazine carts. As these
carts were used also for transporting grain, it excited
remark amongst some Seikhs. The cart in question was
immediately marked in the presence of the Commissariat Establishment, and strict orders were given
that it should not be used again. This shows how careful
we had to be with all the natives about their castes.

In the evening, about dusk, two European artillerymen were struck in the Post-office battery by an 18-
pounder shot, which killed both. Great progress was
made in the battery which was erected by the 13th
Native Infantry, for the 18-pounder to be placed in at the
Baillie Guard gate. Two 8-inch shells exploded in the
vicinity of our magazine, but without doing any injury.
Our third mine from Anderson's house completed, but
not charged, it being retained as a listening gallery.
Another shaft for a mine was struck out from Captain
Saunders's post, to be ready to meet the enemy's so soon
as it could be ascertained which way they were mining.
The cook-boys of two companies of the 32nd Foot
deserted to-day, which caused extreme inconvenience.

2nd September – Sounds of mining heard near the
slaughter-house. This was quite a new direction for the
enemy to commence this work at; but it had not yet been

110 THE DEFENCE OF LUCKNOW

ascertained for a certainty, and appeared most unlikely. Last night three men of Her Majesty's 32nd Regiment died in hospital.

About 9 a.m. this morning a mine of the enemy was discovered within thirty feet of Captain Saunders's post: they came up to a well, and, not knowing what it was, made a hole in the surface; when the smoke from their lamp became apparent. A countermine was immediately commenced and run out sixteen feet, and within two feet of the enemy; it was quickly loaded and tamped for about fourteen feet, and the head of their gallery was blown in. Their miners were heard at work when the hose of our mine was ignited; and it was believed they must have sustained some loss. Another of the enemy's mines was also discovered this morning, coming for the centre of the brigade mess-house; but we had a shaft and gallery ready to frustrate their efforts. One of the sepoys of the 13th Regiment Native Infantry was severely wounded this morning while standing sentry. We had a heavy cannonade from the enemy in the afternoon, and some alteration was made in the position of some of their guns on the Cawnpore side of our position. The advance of a month's pay, which had been offered to all natives, was declined by the 13th, 48th, and 71st, and pensioners, and only four rupees each was received by the Seikh Cavalry, as all preferred to receive it in arrears hereafter. This spoke volumes for their faithfulness.

This evening a very sad event occurred. Lieut. Birch, of the 59th Regiment Native Infantry, attached to the Engineer department, went out at dusk, accompanied by four other officers, to explore some old ruins quite close to the north side of our position, in order to see if there were any traces of mining. The work had been most satisfactorily performed, and the party were returning,

SEPTEMBER 2–3rd 1857

when a sentry of the 32nd Regiment, who, unfortunately, had not received the caution that a party was going out and to be careful not to fire, seeing objects moving in the dark outside our limits, fired his musket; lamentable to relate, it took effect, and the bullet passed through the lower part of the belly of Lieutenant Birch, who died two hours after. He was a gallant and efficient officer, and had only been married six months. His loss was greatly deplored by the garrison. Our miners were all hard at work all day, countermining the enemy, who still persevered in their efforts to blow us up.

September 3rd – About 2 a.m. a very heavy cannonade from the enemy till 9 a.m. Unbarricaded a door leading out of our position, and turned loose during the night sixteen horses and a mule, which had been wounded, and were unfit for use. Further efforts made to limit the supply of flour, and issue wheat in lieu thereof. Advances of pay made to officers, ladies, the civil and uncovenanted service, and a few natives who desired it.

The sun particularly powerful, and as during the nights a heavy dew fell, and occasionally the mornings were very cool, great fears were entertained for the health of our men; especially as nearly all had to sleep in the trenches. Consequently search was everywhere made for tents to shelter them; but the majority of these had been used as barricades and other defences, and were now, from exposure to the rain, &c., completely rotten and useless.

The enemy commenced mining at Sago's garrison, and a shaft and gallery were made to meet them. In the evening there was a heavy cannonade on Mr. Gubbins's post. A soldier of the 32nd was dangerously wounded at Innes's house by an 18-pounder shot, and another

112 THE DEFENCE OF LUCKNOW

slightly wounded by grape shot. Much heavy firing from
the enemy. Very severe work at mining, as our people
were employed at four different points. After 10 p.m. an
exceedingly heavy cannonade accompanied by musketry.
The enemy were distinctly heard repairing their batteries, and moving a heavy gun with elephants, in the
direction of the Cawnpore battery.

September 4th – The usual cannon and musketry
throughout the night, which greatly increased after
daylight, but gradually subsided after 9 a.m.. into a few
solitary discharges of cannon. The outer wall of the mess
house was greatly injured by the constant firing from the
enemy's guns, although it was of great solidity. Between
9 and 10 a.m. an unusual commotion was observable in
the town, and the streets were much crowded, for which
we were unable to account; whatever it was, the crowd
gradually dispersed, and by 11 a.m. all was tranquil, and
the enemy's guards were relieved as usual at that hour.

Towards the middle of the day there was very little
firing from the enemy: they could be distinctly heard in
three of our listening galleries, sapping steadily
towards us. A 32nd soldier was severely contused to-
day by a round shot, while on duty in the Cawnpore
battery, and another wounded by a musket-ball. About
4.30 p.m. Major Bruère, commanding the 13th Regiment Native Infantry, went on the top of the brigade
mess to endeavour to pick off some of the enemy's
gunners. Unfortunately, in his anxiety to get a shot at
some riflemen, he somewhat unnecessarily exposed
himself, and was hit by a rifle-ball through the chest,
which almost immediately proved fatal. His death was
very greatly lamented by the sepoys of the 13th, with
whom he was very popular: they insisted on carrying

SEPTEMBER 4–5th 1857

his remains to the grave, and his funeral was attended by all the men of the 13th who could be permitted to leave their trenches. The eighteen-pounder battery made by the sepoys of the 13th, was now nearly completed, and was sixteen feet thick, besides the wall in front; the eighteen-pounder intended for it was got down, and put in position. The enemy were evidently aware of what we were about, as two shells fell quite close; one just inside, and the other outside the new battery.

The outer wall and buildings on the top of the mess house fell in this evening, with a great crash, consequent on the outer wall having been completely breached; fortunately no one was hurt, and several ladies and children still clung to the inner rooms for shelter, preferring the chance of a round shot or musket-ball to the fetid close atmosphere of an already over-crowded hovel in the interior of our position; which, after all, was perhaps hardly any safer from the fire of the enemy.

September 5th – A fine moonlight morning. Soon after daylight, the enemy commenced the severest cannonade we had yet had. About 8000 infantry and about 500 horse were by sunrise seen moving about round our position, and evidently preparing for an attack. The garrison were soon – every man – on the alert, and remained patiently under a tremendous fire of cannon, awaiting the enemy's onset. They soon opened fire from a new battery of two guns across the river; and about 10 a.m. exploded two mines, one (a large one), close to the 18-pounder battery, and the other, a smaller one, at the brigade-mess (which we had countermined and were about to blow up). Providentially, the enemy had miscalculated their distance in both instances, and were just short of our

114   THE DEFENCE OF LUCKNOW

defences, and neither explosion did us any harm. As soon as the cloud of dust and smoke had cleared away, they advanced under cover of a tremendous fire on several points – particularly at Mr. Gubbins's post – where they came on resolutely and planted an enormous ladder against the bastion to mount it. Several reached the top, but were so steadily received with musketry and hand grenades, that none could gain a footing: and after several leaders had fallen, the rest fell back to the cover of the neighbouring houses, where they kept up a tremendous fire. Their loss was very heavy, as they showed themselves well; particularly in the garden close to the brigade-mess and Sikh square, where they fell rapidly to our rifles and muskets. Long after the action, they could be seen carrying away their killed and wounded over the bridges.

During the attack we only had one havildar of pensioners and two sepoys of the 13th killed, and one soldier of the 32nd wounded (loss of hand), from round shot. Eight sepoys of the 13th Native Infantry, assisted by three artillerymen, loaded and worked the 18-pounder in the 13th battery, and after three or four rounds succeeded in silencing the 18-pounder opposed to them. The sepoys were very proud of this battery, which was entirely under their charge, and constructed solely by them, under the superintendence of the Engineers. A fearfully hot-day, and a broiling sun, to which all were exposed for nearly the entire day. During last night another shaft, eight feet deep, was sunk by the officers of the brigade-mess as a listening gallery, in case the enemy should run a sap in that direction.

In the evening, the enemy seemed disgusted with their want of success in the morning, and confined themselves to a few shots now and then from their batteries. An 18-

The principal street of Lucknow

pounder came right through the hospital from their new work across the river, and passed through the whole length of the building, which was crowded with patients, and very slightly wounded Lieutenant Charlton and a soldier of the 32nd, both of whom were lying there wounded. Passing as it did through the entire length of such a crowded space, it was perfectly extraordinary that this ball did not do more harm.

After all attacks, the enemy were most determined in their efforts to carry off their dead, and generally contrived to do so at night. To-day, as usual, the leading men were most of them knocked over, which greatly discouraged their followers. All reports from positions which commanded any views of the enemy retreating, agreed in saying that they seemed to-day more thoroughly beaten than ever.

116   THE DEFENCE OF LUCKNOW

Lieutenant James Graham, of the 4th Cavalry, shot himself through the head this morning with his revolver, in a fit of temporary insanity: he left a wife and child.

September 6th – At 12 o'clock midnight, the garrison was aroused by a heavy cannonade from all sides, and much bugling and shouting; but it all gradually subsided in about half an hour, without any reply from our side: during it a soldier of the 32nd lost his leg from a round shot. This morning, the enemy were unusually quiet, and their guns more silent than it was remembered for a long time.

The rains seemed to have cleared off; and the sun was most powerful. Our live stock was now fast diminishing in numbers, and had any disease broke out amongst them, it would have been a most serious loss. Our stock of rum and porter was also fast running very low. Now that the stagnant water was fast drying up, the miasmatic stenches in various parts of the garrison were of a morning almost insupportable; and it was greatly feared would produce much fever and other illness. About 1 p.m., the Engineers made a small sortie from Innes's post, and blew down a house which yesterday the enemy commenced to loophole; and which, had they succeeded in doing, would have been a most serious matter to Innes's garrison, in the present shattered and dilapidated state of the house they occupy, caused by the effects of round shot, which had steadily for the last month been fired into it from guns of heavy calibre. Lieutenant Fulton of the Engineers was slightly contused by an explosion to-day. About 10 p.m. the enemy sent two men with loads of combustibles, to place under the entrance gates, to set fire to them; they were seen, and one was shot dead by the sentry, on which the

SEPTEMBER 6–8th 1857

other fled. An hour later, they made a very smart attack on the Baillie Guard gate, but were quickly driven back: during this affair, a very excellent native officer (a subadar), of the 13th Regiment Native Infantry, was killed in the 13th battery.

September 7th – The enemy were unusually quiet with their cannon this morning, contenting themselves with mining, while we as busily endeavoured to countermine them. An unusual commotion among them: large numbers crossing and re-crossing the bridge of boats; and about 11 a.m. a regiment, with colours, and band playing, and about 1000 matchlockmen, passed from right to left of our position. About 5000 men passed during the afternoon from right to left; many of them seemed as though they had marched in from a distance. Heavy showers during the afternoon; the garrison constantly wet.

Our miners, both European and native, were greatly done up with their day and night exertions, which were absolutely requisite for our preservation. In all these operations the Seikhs and Hindoostanee sepoys worked remarkably well.

September 8th – Captain Simons of the Artillery, who had been long suffering from his wounds, died early this morning. A tolerable cannonade kept up all night. The enemy had now completed a breach in the wall enclosing the courtyard of the Martiniere School, broad enough for four or five men to pass through abreast, and which we were obliged to retrench and stockade. Nearly one-half of the officers were on the sick list, with fever and dysentery.

The shot fired in by the enemy were yesterday

118   THE DEFENCE OF LUCKNOW

collected, and 280 round shot, varying in size from a 24 to a 3-pounder, were gathered from the roof of the brigade-mess alone! In the evening we had heavy rain and a moderate cannonade.

September 9th – During the night a shell exploded in a room occupied by a lady and some children, and though almost every article in the room was destroyed, yet all providentially escaped.

Finding this morning that the enemy were rapidly mining towards the Cawnpore battery, it was deemed advisable that our mine, containing 200 lbs. of powder, which had been ready and charged for upwards of a month, should be exploded; and accordingly, at 10 a.m., it was sprung. The effect was tremendous, and it evidently astonished the enemy, whose miners must have been destroyed. They immediately beat to arms, and opened on us from most of their batteries on that side of our position. When the smoke and dust (which were tremendous) had blown away, it was seen that the explosion had destroyed all the front face of the outhouses opposite our battery.

In the evening a body of 3000 men moved up to our right flank, which caused us all to keep particularly on the alert. About 11 p.m. very heavy rain began to fall, and the early part of the night passed away quietly. For the third time since the siege commenced there was no funeral on this day.

September 10th – The rain cleared away towards morning, and all was moderately quiet till 6 a.m., from which hour till 10 a.m. an unusually heavy cannonade was kept up, and replied to by our guns and mortars. All the state jewels were brought over from the Residency,

SEPTEMBER 10–11th 1857

and put into the Begum Kotee for better security.

Owing to the necessity for blowing up the Muchee Bhawun, the officers brought in with them nothing but the clothes they wore. Many others in this garrison had lost everything when their bungalows in cantonments were burnt; and a few better off had shared their wardrobes with them. As time went on, however, clothes wore out, and there were no means of providing others; and by this time officers might have been seen wearing the most extraordinary costumes; few, if any, had any semblance of a military uniform, and very many were in shirts, trowsers, and slippers only; one gallant civilian having found an old billiard-table cloth, had contrived to make himself a kind of loose coat out of it, while an officer wore a shirt made out of a floor cloth. All carried muskets, and were accoutred like the soldiers. At the auction of the effects of an officer recently killed, a single bottle of brandy realised seventeen rupees (thirty-four shillings). The soldiers had for a month past all been out of tobacco, and had taken to smoking dried tea and common leaves. Not very much firing in the evening.

September 11th – This was a quieter night than usual with the garrison. Much disturbance was heard among the enemy, and the noise of elephants was distinctly heard, as if they were moving some of their guns into other positions. About sunrise, two sides of Innes's house, which had been steadily cannonaded daily with 18-pounder shot, fell in, and the two sentries on that side escaped with difficulty; the post was, however, still nobly held, and preparation made for making some kind of a defence out of the debris. Many bodies of armed men were seen moving about, and we had the usual, 'three hours' morning cannonade. About 10 a.m., as our mine out of the Seikh square (which had been charged with 200 lbs. of powder) was ready, it was determined to explode it, as the enemy's miners could be very distinctly heard sapping quite close; it was very successful, completely destroying all their excavations, and buried the party who were at work, the groans and moans of some of whom were heard for some time after. Later in the day, another mine of the enemy was discovered in the church-yard. A sortie was made under Lieutenant Fulton of the Engineers (the ground being open), and the working party were driven off and their work examined. It proved to be shaft and gallery, fully five feet high, and extended twenty-four feet, running in a straight line to the church: two barrels of powder were separately exploded in it, and completely destroyed the entire work. Two of the enemy were shot by Lieutenant Sewell this afternoon.

At dusk, the enemy threw in (apparently from a howitzer) five hollow iron cylinders, filled with a composition (similar to that with which we are accustomed to fill our carcases) done up in strong canvas. On reaching the ground, the apparatus burst, and the five cylinders spouted forth fire without any further explosion: this, perhaps, was the most curious and complicated projectile that had yet been received by the garrison. At 7 p.m. very heavy rain, which lasted an hour and a half.

September 12th – A tremendous row and noise in the city all night. A shaft sunk in the centre of the brigade-mess, in view to running a sap out across the road into the garden, in front of the enemy's battery. Rather less firing all day than usual. Very large bodies of match-lockmen were seen moving about, but a smaller proportion of sepoys. A soldier of the 32nd and an uncovenanted man were wounded; the former in the head, the latter through the hand. During the past few days no case of cholera occurred. In the evening after dark, the 71st sepoys were employed under Lieutenant Langmore in bringing in some tents which were piled up in the Residency garden; while so employed, one of the enemy came up, evidently having mistaken our party for one of his own. He was immediately seized by two sepoys and brought in. An European sentry was killed to-day through a small loophole in the Redan, out of which he was looking, and another in the same battery was wounded during the night.

September 13th – A smart cannonade at daylight. Considerable progress was made in our new mines out of the Cawnpore battery and brigade-mess. Captain Mansfield was seized with cholera early this morning, and died a few hours after. A great number of match-lockmen seen moving about in the bazaar. Enormous prices offered in the garrison for all kinds of supplies. A small fowl was to-day purchased by a gentleman for his sick wife for 20 rupees (2*l*.) A bottle of Curaçoa sold at auction a day or two ago for 16 rupees, and the same price was freely offered for two pounds of sugar. Divine service performed at the brigade-mess, and at Dr. Fayrer's to all who were able to attend. A man came in about 8 p.m. from the city. He could not or would not give any information, was looked upon as a spy, ironed and placed in the main-guard. A tolerably quiet evening.

September 14th – A good many matchlockmen were seen coming into the town during the day, both over the stone bridge and the bridge of boats. For the last two days, the bugles of the enemy had not been beard, which led us to conclude that the headquarters of regiments had probably left the city. A few doolies were seen passing down the Cawnpore road, and a man (apparently of some consequence) was observed haranguing a mob in the city. There was the usual amount of firing and sharp-shooting all day.

A grievous occurrence took place in the afternoon. Lieutenant Fulton of the Engineers, while reconnoitring from a battery in Mr. Gubbins's post, was killed dead by a round shot, which struck him on the head. He had conducted all the engineering operations of the siege for a considerable time previous to the death of his chief (Major Anderson). He was a highly gifted, cool, brave, and chivalrous officer, fertile in resources, and a favour-ite with both officers and men. His loss was acutely felt.

September 15th – The 18-pounder battery beyond Innes's house fired heavily, and reduced Innes's house to almost a heap of ruins; the shot came right across the entire open space round the Residency, and one soldier of the 32nd was mortally and another slightly wounded. The breach in the Seikh square made by the enemy was now tolerably retrenched. The inner square was well loop-holed and barricaded, so that even if the enemy had made their way in, they would have been unable to make a lodgment. The vicinity of the houses to our defences in the outer square rendered mining easy, and we took and blew up three of the enemy's mines at this point alone. Lieutenant Fullerton of the 16th Regiment Native Infantry, died in hospital this morning.

To-day the verandah of the Residency fell in with a great crash, from the effects of the battering it had received from the enemy's 18-pound shot. This after-noon, a mortar, equipped as a howitzer (on Lieutenant

Bonham's principle), was put in position against the 18-pounder battery opposite Innes's house, and fired several shots, which kept the enemy's gun in check; and one shell having blown away most of their parapet, they did not fire again from it during the evening. Under the direction of the garrison engineer, a shaft was commenced in the Baillie Guard gate by the sepoys of 13th Regiment Native Infantry, in order to run a sap out in the direction of the Lutkun Durwaza; eight feet and a half were this evening accomplished. It is intended as a safeguard, to cut off any mine that the enemy may be running towards the gateway.

September 16th – A very sharp cannonade from daylight, for three hours. An 8-inch shell fell in the rear of the 13th battery, (for the second time since the commencement of hostilities) and mortally wounded a sepoy, and slightly wounded a sabadar. Enemy were very busy erecting (apparently) a new battery, to the right of our Cawnpore battery; but it was difficult at the time to say what it was intended for: the people working at it were greatly annoyed by our shells, and it made but little progress, except during the night. They were also very hard at work in front of the Redan battery, where they had made deep trenches in all directions.

Ungud, pensioner and spy, was sent out at about 10 p.m. with a letter, done up in a piece of quill, to take to General Havelock at Cawnpore, and was promised a large reward if he brought a reply. Preparations made for getting the mortar howitzer into the courtyard in rear of the brigade-mess, by cutting a road through the intermediate walls. The mine out of the brigade-mess building, and that out of the Cawnpore battery, were worked all night, and considerable progress was made in

124 THE DEFENCE OF LUCKNOW

both. The rains seemed quite over, the sun was very powerful, and much fever prevailed. Not so much firing as usual in the evening, and only one shell came in. Much bugling among the enemy during the night.

September 17th – All very much as usual, with rather less firing. Many vague rumours were abroad in the garrison; all without foundation. The mortar howitzer was got into position behind the brigade mess; the second shell thrown from it severely wounded two of our servants, in consequence of the shell having exploded before it cleared our defences. After the range was, however, once got, the practice was good, and several shells exploded in the embrasure of the enemy's battery. The mine out of the brigade-mess and that out of the Cawnpore battery, damaged during the day by round shot, was also repaired by a working party of sepoys from the 48th regiment Native Infantry. The sentry of the 32nd Foot, on duty at the church, had his head carried off by a round shot. Exactly at midnight the enemy made a demonstration on Saunders's post, and fired heavy volleys of musketry, but made no attempt to advance; in about half an hour, after a few shells had been thrown among them, they retired.

Many cases of fever and dysentery. Two sepoys of the 13th died in hospital of their wounds. The Seikh cavalry sowars, under Lieutenant Hardinge, worked at the barricade across the breach in the third Seikh square, and still further strengthened it.

September 18th – Nothing new to record. Each day passed away much like its predecessor, with the same amount of cannonading and musketry fire.

Throughout the siege, a regular system of look-out was

organised from the top of the tower in the Residency, which commanded a view of the river, the three bridges, and the open country beyond; and also from the roof of the Post-office, from which a great part of the city and the road to Cawnpore could be observed. At the former post the officers were relieved every two hours, and at the latter hourly. At each post a book was kept, in which whatever had been observed was noted down, and if anything unusual, or any new work of the enemy was seen, a report of it was instantly forwarded for Brigadier Inglis's information. A new truck was constructed to enable us to fit out another mortar as a howitzer, for it would be impossible to say how greatly we felt throughout the siege the want of a couple of 8-inch howitzers. To-day, the enemy threw in (evidently from a 13-inch mortar) a piece of wood of very great weight, which measured twelve inches in diameter and eighteen in length! It made a prodigious noise as it passed through the air.

In consequence of the very small stock of rum left in store, all the Europeans were reduced to one dram each per day. This was perhaps the quietest day of the siege up to this date, as we had nothing but a few stray cannon shots and a slight musketry fire throughout the twenty-four hours. About 11 p.m. a very considerable noise was heard in the town, together with much bugling and shouting.

September 19th – This morning, almost before day-light, we commenced a heavy cannonade from the Post-office on the battery in the square house opposite. During the morning the enemy kept up also a heavy fire all around; particularly on the Residency, which now wore a most desolate tumble-down and dilapidated appearance,

126   THE DEFENCE OF LUCKNOW

from the effect of round shot which had been steadily poured into it daily from the commencement of the siege. About 10.30 a.m. the enemy's battery in the square house, opposite the Post-office was set on fire by our shot, and a pretty sharp fusillade and cannonade was kept up by us to prevent the enemy from distinguishing it; the fire however soon died out. An auction was held this day in the Residency of the property (clothes, &c.) of deceased officers, and the prices that all useful articles fetched was enormous: for instance, a new flannel shirt was knocked down for forty rupees, while five old ones were sold for 112 rupees, and a bottle of brandy brought twenty rupees. A man of the 84th was shot dead at Sago's post early this morning. During the day the enemy threw into our position, probably from an enormous mortar, six pieces of wood about the size and shape of a large oyster barrel; they were thrown up in the air to an enormous height, and came down with almost incredible force.

September 20th – At 1 a.m. a smart musketry fire and cannonade took place, which lasted for about half an hour. At daylight discovered two new batteries, which the enemy had very nearly completed, and one of which contained a 32-pounder. We opened on them with a howitzer and an 18-pounder, but did them little mischief; the batteries having been made excessively strong, with enormous beams of wood and earth. We however, entirely prevented them from working at either battery during the ensuing night. The Cawnpore battery was repaired, and the centre mine from the brigade mess was connected with the one we had previously run out from the left. The guard-room at Anderson's house was lowered by digging out the floor, so as to keep the guard clear of the round shot which passed through it; the 13th

SEPTEMBER 20–21st 1857

mine was also worked eighteen feet further. A very considerable noise was heard in the city for some hours after dark. During the day nearly as many men as usual seen moving about. A private of Her Majesty's 32nd at Innes's post was killed by a round shot.

September 21st – Between 12 and 1 o'clock a.m. the enemy suddenly began a very smart musketry fire all along the city side of our position, and opened from their guns. We threw a few shells amongst them, and their fire soon subsided into the usual steady fire which had gone on every night of the siege.

About 4 a.m., we had very heavy rain which lasted till about 11 a.m. The heavy rain seemed to keep the enemy quiet, and there was little firing on either side till 1 p.m., when one of our 18-pounders at the Post-office opened on the enemy's new 32-pounder battery, and knocked their parapet about, leaving the gun greatly exposed; which enabled Captain Saunders's garrison to pick off two of the enemy's gunners at the gun, and keep it silent for the rest of the day. In the afternoon, the enemy battered down a great portion of the wall enclosing the building occupied by the Martiniere school-boys, and killed a water-carrier who was drawing water at the time, and who was knocked dead into the well; which was a great misfortune, as none of the natives would again use it. The body was got up soon after. Not many armed men were seen in the morning beyond the enemy's regular relief of guards and pickets. At 10 p.m. heavy rain came on. About 11 p.m. the enemy were reported to be in unusual strength near the Seikh square, on which all were kept well on the alert. A shell was thrown among them, but nothing further took place.

*

September 22nd – Continued heavy rain, which fell without cessation till about 3 p.m. The garrison were in a great state of discomfort, as little shelter was to be had anywhere; the roofs of all the buildings were so injured from eighty-four days' constant cannonading that but few could boast of a waterproof residence. Lieutenant Cunliffe of the Artillery, died early this morning from fever; he had previously been wounded. A Seikh sepoy of the 13th, a native artilleryman, two private servants, and three grass-cutters deserted during the night; and in the course of the morning four cook boys contrived to desert during the heavy rain. The rain did considerable damage to various parts of our defences, washing down many of the fascines in the batteries, and causing several parts of the defences at Mr. Gubbins's and Innes's post to fall down. A great part of the outside wall of the brigade mess also fell from the same cause. Towards evening the enemy opened their guns, and we dismounted one of their 9-pounders by a shell, which fell on the top of one of them and killed two gunners. About 11 p.m. Ungud, pensioner, returned, bringing us a letter containing the glad tidings that our relieving force, under General Outram, had crossed the Ganges, and would arrive in a few days. His arrival, and the cheering news he brought of speedy aid, was well-timed; for neither our fast diminishing stores, the vague and uncertain rumours of the advent of reinforcements, nor the daily sights and sounds by which we were surrounded, were calculated to inspire confidence and check desertion among the servants and camp followers. All the garrison were greatly elated with the news, and on many of the sick and wounded, the speedy prospect of a change of air and security exercised a most beneficial effect. Heavy rain fell about 11 p.m.

SEPTEMBER 23–24th 1857

September 23rd – About 3 a.m. the rain cleared off, and at 11 a.m. the sun came out and the clouds dispersed, and gave promise of fair weather. A smart cannonade was heard in the direction of Cawnpore; several imagined they also heard musketry, and the sound was listened to with the most intense and even painful anxiety by the garrison, who felt assured it must be their friends advancing to their assistance. But it was hardly expected that our force could have advanced so far, owing to the heavy rain which had fallen, and the state in consequence that the roads and country were in; however at 5 p.m. another distant cannonade was heard which lasted for half an hour, and which appeared much nearer than before: this elicited many and divers opinions, and created the greatest possible excitement.

Throughout the day, large bodies of troops with guns and ammunition waggons were seen moving about in the city, in the early part of the day to the right, and later, in large bodies to the left. In the afternoon, the enemy placed a gun in position facing down the Kass bazaar street, with what object it was impossible to say. We threw many shells into the city during the day among the parties of the enemy seen moving about. At 9 p.m. heavy rain began and fell for two hours.

September 24th – Everything most unusually quiet throughout the night, and only one or two cannon shot were fired early in the morning. A considerable body of cavalry were seen moving to the right through the city, and about 8.30 a.m. a distant cannonade was heard, which continued nearly all day.

We had no news of any kind, and the anxiety of the garrison was very great. During the morning, large bodies of the enemy were seen moving through the city to

130 THE DEFENCE OF LUCKNOW

the right and left. Ensign Hewitt, of the 41st Regiment Native Infantry, was slightly contused on the head by bricks struck out of a wall by a round shot. At 8 p.m. the enemy made a false attack on the Cawnpore battery, keeping up a heavy cannonade and musketry fire which lasted for about half an hour, after which all became moderately quiet. During the night guns were heard in the direction of the Cawnpore road, and the flash of them could be very distinctly seen; they were supposed to be about seven miles distant.

September 25th – A very unquiet night. Two alarms, one at 1.30 a.m. and another at 4 a.m. The whole garrison were under arms nearly the whole night. A very great disturbance in the city, in the direction of Mr. Gubbins's post especially. To the very great regret of the garrison, Captain Radcliffe of the 7th Light Cavalry was dangerously wounded while in command of the Cawnpore battery. About 10 a.m. a messenger came in bringing in a letter of the 16th instant from General Outram, dated Cawnpore, announcing his being about to cross over to this side of the Ganges, and march on to Lucknow. The messenger could give no account of our force, beyond its having reached the outskirts of the city.

About 11 a.m. nearly all sound of firing had ceased, but increased agitation was visible among the people in the town, in which two large fires were seen. An hour later, the sound of musketry and the smoke of guns was distinctly perceived within the limits of the city. All the garrison was on the alert, and the excitement amongst many of the officers and soldiers was quite painful to witness. At 1.30 p.m. many of the people of the city commenced leaving, with bundles of clothes, &c. on their

SEPTEMBER 25th 1857

heads, and took the direction of cantonments across the different bridges. At 2 p.m. armed men and sepoys commenced to follow them, accompanied by large bodies of Irregular Cavalry. Every gun and mortar that could be brought to bear on the evidently retreating enemy, was fired as fast as possible, for at least an hour and a half. The enemy's bridge of boats had evidently been destroyed and broken away, for many were seen swimming across the river, most of them cavalry with their horses' bridles in their hands. Strange to relate, during all this apparent panic, the guns of the enemy in position all round us kept up a heavy cannonade, and the matchlockmen or riflemen never ceased firing from their respective loop-holes.

At 4 p.m. report was made that some officers dressed in shooting coats and solah caps, a regiment of Europeans in blue pantaloons and shirts, and a bullock battery were seen near Mr. Martin's house and the Motee Muhal. At 5 p.m. volleys of musketry, rapidly growing louder, were heard in the city. But soon the firing of a minié ball over our heads gave notice of the still nearer approach of our friends; of whom as yet little or nothing had been seen, though the enemy were to be seen firing heavily on them from many of the roofs of the houses. Five minutes later, and our troops were seen fighting their way through one of the principal streets; and though men fell at almost every step, yet nothing could withstand the headlong gallantry of our reinforcements. Once fairly SEEN, all our doubts and fears regarding them were ended: and then the garrison's long pent-up feelings of anxiety and suspense burst forth in a succession of deafening cheers; from every pit, trench and battery – from behind the sandbags piled on shattered houses – from every post still held by a few

132 THE DEFENCE OF LUCKNOW

gallant spirits, rose cheer on cheer – even from the hospital! Many of the wounded crawled forth to join in that glad shout of welcome to those who had so bravely come to our assistance. It was a moment never to be forgotten.

Soon all the rearguard and heavy guns were inside our position; and then ensued a scene which baffles description. For eighty-seven days the Lucknow garrison had lived in utter ignorance of all that had taken place outside. Wives who had long mourned their husbands as dead, were again restored to them; others, fondly looking forward to glad meetings with those near and dear to them, now for the first time learnt that they were alone. On all sides eager inquiries for relations and friends were made. Alas! in too many instances the answer was a painful one

The force under the command of General Sir James Outram, G.C.B., came to our assistance at a heavy sacrifice to themselves. Of 2600 who left Cawnpore, nearly one-third was either killed or wounded in forcing their way through the city: indeed, the losses were so heavy that they could effect nothing towards our relief; as the enemy were in overpowering force, and the position having been extended, in order to accommodate as far as possible our great increase in numbers, and the guns that were in our vicinity having been captured at considerable loss to ourselves, we remained on three-quarter rations, as closely besieged as before, until the 22nd November; when the garrison were finally relieved by the army under the Commander-in-Chief.

Appendix

No. I

Captain Radcliffe's (7th Light Cavalry) Narrative

On the evening of the 30th May, about 9 o'clock, shots were heard at Moodkeepore (the cavalry station), in the direction of the infantry lines in Lucknow. The 7th Cavalry, consisting of about 150 sabres, immediately were turned out by their officers, and placed in three troops. On wheeling into line, about 30 men rushed out of the ranks, and rode furiously towards cantonments: they were not seen again. The corps advanced towards the race-course, towards the Residency, at a canter, which place they reached about half-past 9 or a quarter to 10. The regiment received orders to patrol round the Residency, and in the rear of Colonel Halford's house, which was done accordingly, and they afterwards formed up in rear of the lines stationed on the city road.

About 11 o'clock the 7th Cavalry marched down to the Baillie Guard, patrolled towards Muchee Bhawun, and, finding all safe, returned *viâ* the stone bridge through Mukka Gunge, warned all on duty at the elephant sheds to be on the alert, and reached the Residency in cantonments about 2 in the morning. At 3 o'clock the 4th troop arrived from Chinhut, under the command of Captain T. Boileau. At a quarter after gunfire the cavalry marched off with the two artillery guns from the Residency, and took up a position on the right of the line on the 32nd

134 THE DEFENCE OF LUCKNOW

parade ground. The 7th were directed to move towards Moodkeepore, which place was reported to have fallen into the hands of the mutineers. The corps advanced at a canter, and on reaching the plain close to the race-course, a large body of armed infantry, amounting to some 1000 men, were seen advancing in skirmishing order towards the cavalry. The report was, as regarded Moodkeepore, too true, for the Standard Guard was looted, public and private property destroyed, and the 2nd Squadron standard was actually seized from the hands of the jemadar in charge, and dashed to pieces.

Lieutenant Raleigh, who had lately joined the corps, was brutally murdered at 5 a.m. in front of the first troop lines. This officer was sick, and unable to join the regiment the night before when ordered out. The officer commanding ordered his men to form line to the front, which was done rather sullenly; but on his ordering the line to take ground to the right, a number of men broke out from the ranks, crying out that they *would* charge, as their children, etc., were being murdered; they rode away towards the mutineers, having been beckoned to come over by a leader riding a horse and bearing a standard. Some thirty-five or forty men left their officers. At this time an officer was sent back towards cantonments to request Sir Henry Lawrence to send up some guns, as the small body of cavalry that were left alone in front of the insurgents were in danger of being driven back.

The guns soon afterwards came up, and after a few rounds dispersed the enemy. The 7th Cavalry, in concert with the Irregulars, followed up the retreating mutineers, killed one or two, and sent in some ten or twelve prisoners. The corps returned to Moodkeepore about 10 o'clock, and marched into cantonments in the evening, and took up a position on the right of the line. Some 105

APPENDIX I

men remained with their officers up to the 12th June, on which date, by authority, they were given two months' pay, and allowed a furlough to their homes till the 15th October. The men remaining after the mutiny behaved admirably in quarters, and when told they were to go to their homes obeyed the order, quietly lodging their arms, and moving quietly homewards. The horses of the corps were marched down to the Residency at noon of the 12th, and in the evening the European and native officers, with the standards, repaired to the Baillie Guard, opposite to which the cavalry horses were ordered to be picketed.

No. II

*Account of the Explosion at the Seikh Square
on 18th of August*

(Dated) Lucknow, 19th August, 1857

YESTERDAY morning, between the hours of 5 and 6, the enemy sprung a mine at the Seikh Square, blowing down the corner house, on the top of which Lieutenant Mecham and Captain Orr, with two sentries, were on the look out from the loopholes, Lieutenant Soppitt being below at the time.

A few minutes before the explosion not a single individual was to be seen in the quarter occupied by the enemy. Suddenly, however, one man was discovered by a sentry, and Lieutenant Mecham fired at him, but missed; and immediately after the mine exploded, sending four of us, viz., Lieutenant Mechan, Band-sergeant Curtain, of the 41st Native Infantry, Drummer Ford, of the 13th Native Infantry, and Captain Orr up in the air, and burying underneath the ruins of the battery six drummers and one Sepoy, *i.e.,* Wiltshire, Williams, 13th Native Infantry, E. Curtain, A. Nugent, Rowlan, 41st Native Infantry, Fife-major Shipley, 4th Oude Irregular Force, and sepoy Heerah Sing, 48th Regiment Native Infantry. Of the former, I regret to state that Band-sergeant Curtain was thrown on the enemy's side and killed; Lieutenant Mecham and Drummer Ford were almost unhurt, and Captain Orr escaped with a few bruises.

Every precaution had been taken by Lieutenants

APPENDIX II 137

Mecham, Soppitt, and Captain Orr to guard against all contingencies, Lieutenant Mecham remaining at night with the sentries, Lieutenant Soppitt and Captain Orr being below with the guard, and occasionally visiting the sentries. Since on duty at the Seikh Battery we had already discovered two mines, one of which we countermined, and the other we found to be an abortive attempt at one. The above discoveries had the effect of making us doubly vigilant on this point.

The new mine, which occasioned the calamity of yesterday, must have been worked by the enemy with sharp and noiseless tools; as – though a shaft was already sunk beneath the battery, over which a sentry was posted, and into which, during our respective tour of duty, we each occasionally descended for the purpose of listening whether mining was carried on by the enemy – not the slightest sound which in any way led us to suppose the same was the case, ever reached us.

There was never perfect silence in the square, owing to the Seikhs' horses being picketed therein, the tramping of whose feet on the ground had more than once previously deceived us.

The smoke and dust thrown up enveloping us for some moments in complete darkness, and the sudden shock of the explosion, prevented my personally knowing what subsequently happened.

No. III

*Division Orders by Major-General
Sir J. Outram, G.C.B.*

Head Quarters, Lucknow, 5th October, 1857

THE incessant and arduous duties which have devolved on Brigadier Inglis and his staff, since the arrival of the relieving force, had hitherto prevented him from furnishing to the Major-General Commanding the usual official documents relative to the siege of the garrison.

In the absence of these the Major-General could not, with propriety, have indulged in any public declaration of the admiration with which he regards the heroism displayed by Brigadier Inglis and the glorious garrison he has so ably commanded during the last three months, and he has been reluctantly obliged therefore to defer so long the expression of the sentiments he was desirous to offer.

But the Major-General having at length received Brigadier Inglis's reports, is relieved from the necessity of further silence, and he hastens to tender to the Brigadier, and to every individual member of the garrison, the assurance of his confidence that their services will be regarded by the Government under which they are immediately serving, by the British nation, and by Her Gracious Majesty, with equal admiration to that with which he is himself impressed.

The Major-General believes that the annals of warfare contain no brighter page than that which will record the

APPENDIX III   139

bravery, fortitude, vigilance, and patient endurance of
hardships, privation, and fatigue, displayed by the
garrison of Lucknow; and he is very conscious that his
unskilled pen must needs fail adequately to convey to the
Right Honourable the Governor-General of India, and
his Excellency the Commander-in-Chief, the profound
sense of the merits of that garrison which has been forced
on his mind by a careful consideration of the almost
incredible difficulties with which they have had to
contend.

The term 'illustrious' was well and happily applied by
a former Governor-General of India to the garrison of
Jellalabad; but some far more laudatory epithet – if such
the English language contains – is due, the Major-
General considers, to the brave men whom Brigadier
Inglis has commanded with undeviating success and
untarnished honour through the late memorable siege.
For while the devoted hand of heroes who so nobly
maintained the honour of their country's arms under Sir
R. Sale were seldom exposed to actual attack, the Lucknow garrison, of inferior strength, have, in addition to a
series of fierce assaults, gallantly and successfully repulsed, been for three months exposed to a nearly incessant fire from strong and commanding positions, held by
an enemy of overwhelming force, possessing powerful artillery, having at their command the whole resources of
what was but recently a kingdom, and animated by an
insane and bloodthirsty fanaticism.

It is a source of heartfelt satisfaction to the Major-
General to be able, to a certain extent, to confer on the
native portion of the garrison an instalment of those
rewards which their gallant and grateful commander
has sought for them, and which he is very certain the Governor-General will bestow in full; and though the

140   THE DEFENCE OF LUCKNOW

Major-General, as regards the European portion of the garrison, cannot do more than give his most earnest and hearty support to the recommendations of the Brigadier, he feels assured that the Governor-General of India will fully and publicly manifest his appreciation of their distinguished services, and that our beloved Sovereign will herself deign to convey to them some gracious expression of royal approbation of their conduct.

Brigadier Inglis has borne generous testimony to the bravery, vigilance, devotedness, and good conduct of all ranks; and to all ranks, as the local representative of the British Indian Government, the Major-General tenders his warmest acknowledgments, – he would fain offer his special congratulations and thanks to the European and Eurasian portion of the garrison whom Brigadier Inglis has particularly noticed, but, by doing so, he would forestall the Governor-General in the exercise of what, the Major-General is assured, will be one of the most pleasing acts of his official life.

No. IV

*From Brigadier Inglis, Commanding Garrison of
Lucknow, to the Secretary to Government Military
Department, Calcutta*

Lucknow, September 26th, 1857

SIR,

In consequence of the very deeply-to-be-lamented
death of Brigadier-General Sir H. M. Lawrence, K.C.B.,
late in command of the Oude Field Force, the duty of
narrating the military events which have occurred at
Lucknow since the 29th of June last has devolved upon
myself.

On the evening of that day several reports reached Sir
Henry Lawrence that the rebel army, in no very
considerable force, would march from Chinhut (a small
village about eight miles distant, on the road to Fyzabad)
on Lucknow on the following morning; and the late
Brigadier-General therefore determined to make a
strong reconnaissance in that direction, with the view, if
possible, of meeting the force at a disadvantage, either at
its entrance into the suburbs of the city, or at the bridge
across the Gokral, which is a small stream intersecting
Fyzabad road, midway between Lucknow and Chinhut.

The force destined for this service, and which was
composed as follows, moved out at 6 a.m. on the morning
of the 30th of June: –

Artillery – Four guns of No. – Horse Light Field
Battery, four guns of No.2 Oude Field Battery, two guns
of No. 3 Oude Field Battery, and an 8-inch howitzer.

Cavalry – Troop of Volunteer Cavalry, and 120

troopers of detachments belonging to the 1st, 2nd, and 3rd Regiments of Oude Irregular Cavalry.

Infantry – Three hundred of Her Majesty's 32nd, 150 of the 13th Native Infantry, 60 of the 48th Native Infantry, and 20 of the 71st Native Infantry (Sikhs).

The troops, misled by the reports of wayfarers – who stated that there were few or no men between Lucknow and Chinhut – proceeded somewhat farther than had been originally intended, and suddenly fell in with the enemy, who had up to that time eluded the vigilance of the advanced guard, by concealing themselves behind a long line of trees in overwhelming numbers. The European force and the howitzer, with the native infantry, held the foe in check for some time, and had the six guns of the Oude Artillery been faithful, and the Sikh cavalry shown a better front, the day would have been won, in spite of an immense disparity in numbers. But the Oude artillerymen and drivers were traitors. They overturned the guns into ditches, cut the traces of their horses, and abandoned them, regardless of the remonstrances and exertions of their own officers, and of those of Sir Henry Lawrence's staff, headed by the Brigadier-General in person, who himself drew his sword upon these rebels. Every effort to induce them to stand having proved ineffectual, the force, exposed to a vastly superior fire of artillery, and completely outflanked on both sides by an overpowering body of infantry and cavalry, which actually got into our rear, was compelled to retire with the loss of three pieces of artillery, which fell into the hands of the enemy, in consequence of the rank treachery of the Oude gunners, and with a very grievous list of killed and wounded. The heat was dreadful, the gun ammunition was expended, and the almost total want of cavalry to protect our rear made our retreat most disastrous.

APPENDIX IV 143

All the officers behaved well, and the exertions of the small body of Volunteer Cavalry – only forty in number – under Captain Radcliffe, 7th Light Cavalry, were most praiseworthy. Sir Henry Lawrence subsequently conveyed his thanks to myself, who had, at his request, accompanied him upon this occasion (Colonel Case being in command of Her Majesty's 32nd). He also expressed his approbation of the way in which his Staff – Captain Wilson, officiating deputy assistant adjutant-general; Lieutenant James, sub-assistant commissary-general; Captain Edgel, officiating military secretary; and Mr. Couper, C.S. – the last of whom had acted as Sir Henry Lawrence's A.D.C. from the commencement of the disturbances, – had conducted themselves throughout this arduous day. Sir Henry further particularly mentioned that he would bring the gallant conduct of Captain Radcliffe and of Lieutenant Bonham, of the Artillery, (who worked the howitzer successfully until incapacitated by a wound,) to the prominent notice of the Government of India. The manner in which Lieutenant Birch, 71st Native Infantry, cleared a village with a party of Sikh skirmishes, also elicited the admiration of the Brigadier-General. The conduct of Lieutenant Hardinge, who, with his handful of horse, covered the retreat of the rear-guard, was extolled by Sir Henry, who expressed his intention of mentioning the services of this gallant officer to his Lordship in Council. Lieutenant-Colonel Case, who commanded Her Majesty's 32nd Regiment, was mortally wounded whilst gallantly leading on his men. The service had not a more deserving officer. The command devolved on Captain Steevens, who also received a death-wound shortly afterwards. The command then fell to Captain Mansfield, who has since died of cholera.

144   THE DEFENCE OF LUCKNOW

It will be in the recollection of his Lordship in Council that it was the original intention of Sir Henry Lawrence to occupy not only the Residency, but also the fort called Muchee Bhawun – an old dilapidated edifice, which had been hastily repaired for the occasion, though the defences were, even at the last moment, very far from complete, and were, moreover, commanded by many houses in the city. The situation of the Muchee Bhawun, with regard to the Residency, has already been described to the Government of India.

The untoward event of June the 30th so far diminished the whole available force that we had not a sufficient number of men remaining to occupy both positions. The Brigadier-General, therefore, on the evening of July the 1st signalled to the garrison of the Muchee Bhawun to evacuate and blow up that fortress in the course of the night. The orders were ably carried out, and at 12 p.m. the force marched into the Residency, with their guns and treasure, without the loss of a man; and shortly afterwards the explosion of 240 barrels of gunpowder and 6,000,000 ball cartridges, which were lying in the magazine, announced to Sir Henry Lawrence and his officers, who were anxiously awaiting the report, the complete destruction of that post and all that it contained. If it had not been for this wise and strategic measure, no member of the Lucknow garrison, in all probability, would have survived to tell the tale; for, as has already been stated, the Muchee Bhawun was commanded from other parts of the town, and was, moreover, indifferently provided with heavy artillery ammunition; while the difficulty, suffering, and loss which the Residency garrison, even with the re-inforcement thus obtained from the Muchee Bhawun, has undergone in holding the position, is sufficient to

APPENDIX IV

145

show that if the original intention of holding both posts had been adhered to, both would have inevitably fallen.

It is now my very painful duty to relate the calamity which befell us at the commencement of the siege. On the 1st July an 8-inch shell burst in the room in the Residency in which Sir H. Lawrence was sitting. The missile burst between him and Mr. Couper, close to both; but without injury to either. The whole of his staff implored Sir Henry to take up other quarters, as the Residency had then become the special target for the round shot and shell of the enemy. This, however, he jestingly declined to do, observing that another shell would certainly never be pitched into that small room. But Providence had ordained otherwise, for on the very next day he was mortally wounded by the fragment of another shell which burst in the same room exactly at the same spot. Captain Wilson, deputy assistant adjutant-general, received a contusion at the same time.

The late lamented Sir H. Lawrence, knowing that his last hour was rapidly approaching, directed me to assume command of the troops, and appointed Major Banks to succeed him in the office of Chief Commissioner. He lingered in great agony till the morning of the 4th July, when he expired, and the Government was thereby deprived, if I may venture to say so, of the services of a distinguished statesman and a most gallant soldier. Few men have ever possessed to the same extent the power he enjoyed of winning the hearts of all those with whom he came in contact, and thus ensuring the warmest and most zealous devotion for himself and for the Government which he served. The successful defence of the position has been, under Providence, solely attributable to the foresight which be evinced in the timely commencement of the necessary operations, and

146 THE DEFENCE OF LUCKNOW

the great skill and untiring personal activity which he exhibited in carrying them into effect. All ranks possessed such confidence in his judgment and his fertility of resource, that the news of his fall was received throughout the garrison with feelings of consternation only second to the grief which was inspired in the hearts of all by the loss of a public benefactor and a warm personal friend. Feeling as keenly and as gratefully as I do the obligations that the whole of us are under to this great and good man, I trust the Government of India will pardon me for having attempted, however imperfectly, to portray them. In him every good and deserving soldier lost a friend and a chief capable of discriminating, and ever on the alert to reward merit, no matter how humble the sphere in which it was exhibited.

The garrison had scarcely recovered the shock which it had sustained in the loss of its revered and beloved General, when it had to mourn the death of that able and respected officer, Major Banks, the officiating chief commissioner, who received a bullet through his head while examining a critical outpost on the 21st July, and died without a groan. The description of our position, and the state of our defences when the siege began, are so fully set forth in the memorandum furnished by the garrison engineer, that I shall content myself with bringing to the notice of his Lordship in Council the fact that when the blockade was commenced, only two of our batteries were completed, part of the defences were yet in an unfinished condition, and the buildings in the immediate vicinity, which gave cover to the enemy, were only very partially cleared away. Indeed, our heaviest losses have been caused by the fire from the enemy's sharpshooters stationed in the adjoining mosques and houses of the native nobility, the necessity of destroying which had

APPENDIX IV

147

been repeatedly drawn to the attention of Sir Henry by the staff of engineers. But his invariable reply was, 'Spare the holy places, and private property too, as much as possible;' and we have consequently suffered severely from our very tenderness to the religious prejudices and respect to the rights of our rebellious citizens and soldiery. As soon as the enemy had thoroughly completed the investment of the Residency, they occupied these houses, some of which were within easy pistol-shot of our barricades, in immense force, and rapidly made loopholes on those sides which bore on our post, from which they kept up a terrific and incessant fire day and night, which caused many daily casualties, as there could not have been less than 8,000 men firing at one time into our position. Moreover, there was no place in the whole of our works that could be considered safe, for several of the sick and wounded who were lying in the banquetting hall, which had been turned into a hospital, were killed in the very centre of the building, and the widow of Lieutenant Dorin and other women and children were shot dead in rooms into which it had not been previously deemed possible that a bullet could penetrate. Neither were the enemy idle in erecting batteries. They soon had from twenty to twenty-five guns in position, some of them of very large calibre. These were planted all round our post at small distances, some being actually within fifty yards of our defences, but in places where our own heavy guns could not reply to them, while the perseverance and ingenuity of the enemy in erecting barricades in front of and around, their guns in a very short time, rendered all attempts to silence them by musketry unavailing. Neither could they be effectually silenced by shells, by reason of their extreme proximity to our position, and because, moreover, the enemy had

148 THE DEFENCE OF LUCKNOW

recourse to digging very narrow trenches about eight feet in depth in rear of each gun, in which the men lay while our shells were flying, and which so effectually concealed them, even while working the gun, that our baffled sharpshooters could only see their hands while in the act of loading.

The enemy contented themselves with keeping up this incessant fire of cannon and musketry until the 20th July, on which day, at 10 a.m., they assembled in very great force all round our position, and exploded a heavy mine inside our outer line of defences at the Water Gate. The mine, however, which was close to the Redan, and apparently sprung with the intention of destroying that battery, did no harm. But as soon as the smoke had cleared away, the enemy boldly advanced under cover of a tremendous fire of cannon and musketry, with the object of storming the Redan. But they were received with such a heavy fire, that after a short struggle they fell back with much loss. A strong column advanced at the same time to attack Innes's post, and came on to within ten yards of the palisades, affording to Lieutenant Loughnan, 13th Native Infantry, who commanded the position, and his brave garrison, composed of gentlemen of the Uncovenanted Service, a few of Her Majesty's 32nd Foot and the 13th Native Infantry, an opportunity of distinguishing themselves, which they were not slow to avail themselves of, and the enemy were driven back with great slaughter. The insurgents made minor attacks at almost every outpost, but were invariably defeated, and at 2 p.m. they ceased their attempts to storm the place, although their musketry fire and cannonading continued to harass us unceasingly as usual. Matters proceeded in this manner until the 10th August, when the enemy made another assault, having

APPENDIX IV

previously sprung a mine close to the brigade mess, which entirely destroyed our defences for the space of twenty feet, and blew in a great portion of the outside wall of the house occupied by Mr. Shilling's garrison. On the dust clearing away, a breach appeared, through which a regiment could have advanced in perfect order, and a few of the enemy came on with the utmost determination, but were met with such a withering flank fire of musketry from the officers and men holding the top of the brigade mess, that they beat a speedy retreat, leaving the more adventurous of their numbers lying on the crest of the breach. While this operation was going on, another large body advanced on the Cawnpore battery, and succeeded in locating themselves for a few minutes in the ditch. They were, however, dislodged by hand-grenades. At Captain Anderson's post they also came boldly forward with scaling ladders, which they planted against the wall; but here, as elsewhere, they were met with the most indomitable resolution, and the leaders being slain, the rest fled, leaving the ladders, and retreated to their batteries and loopholed defences, from whence they kept up, for the rest of the day, an unusually heavy cannonade and musketry fire. On the 18th August the enemy sprung another mine in front of the Sikh lines with very fatal effect. Captain Orr (unattached), Lieutenants Mecham and Soppitt, who commanded the small body of drummers composing the garrison, were blown into the air; but providentially returned to earth with no further injury than a severe shaking. The garrison, however, were not so fortunate. No less than eleven men were buried alive under the ruins, from whence it was impossible to extricate them, owing to the tremendous fire kept up by the enemy from houses situated not ten yards in front of the breach. The

150   THE DEFENCE OF LUCKNOW

explosion was followed by a general assault of a less determined nature than the two former efforts, and the enemy were consequently repulsed without much difficulty. But they succeeded, under cover of the breach, in establishing themselves in one of the houses in our position, from which they were driven in the evening by the bayonets of Her Majesty's 32nd and 84th Foot. On the 5th of September the enemy made their last serious assault. Having exploded a large mine, a few feet short of the bastion of the 18-pounder gun, in Major Apthorp's post, they advanced with large heavy scaling ladders, which they planted against the wall, and mounted, thereby gaining for an instant the embrasure of a gun. They were, however, speedily driven back with loss by hand-grenades and musketry. A few minutes subsequently they sprung another mine close to the brigade mess, and advanced boldly; but soon the corpses strewed in the garden in front of the post bore testimony to the fatal accuracy of the rifle and musketry fire of the gallant members of that garrison, and the enemy fled ignominiously, leaving their leader − a fine-looking old native officer − among the slain. At other posts they made similar attacks, but with less resolution, and everywhere with the same want of success. Their loss upon this day must have been very heavy, as they came on with much determination, and at night they were seen bearing large numbers of their killed and wounded over the bridges in the direction of cantonments.

The above is a faint attempt at a description of the four great struggles which have occurred during this protracted season of exertion, exposure, and suffering. His Lordship in Council will perceive that the enemy invariably commenced his attacks by the explosion of a mine, − a species of offensive warfare, for the exercise of which

APPENDIX IV   151

our position was unfortunately peculiarly situated; and
had it not been for the most untiring vigilance on our
part, in watching and blowing up their mines before they
were completed, the assaults would probably have been
much more numerous, and might, perhaps, have ended
in the capture of the place. But by countermining in all
directions, we succeeded in detecting and destroying no
less than four of the enemy's subterraneous advances
towards important positions, two of which operations
were eminently successful, as on one occasion not less
than eighty of them were blown into the air, and twenty
suffered a similar fate on the second explosion. The
labour, however, which devolved upon us in making
these counter-mines, in the absence of a body of skilled
miners, was very heavy. The Right Honourable the
Governor-General in Council will feel that it would be
impossible to crowd, within the limits of a despatch, even
the principal events, much more the individual acts of
gallantry, which have marked this protracted struggle.
But I can conscientiously declare my conviction, that few
troops have ever undergone greater hardships, exposed
as they have been to a never-ceasing musketry fire and
cannonade. They have also experienced the alternate
vicissitudes of extreme wet and intense heat, and that
too with very insufficient shelter from either, and in
many places without any shelter at all. In addition to
having to repel real attacks, they have been exposed
night and day to the hardly less harassing false alarms
which the enemy have been constantly raising. The
insurgents have frequently fired very heavily, sounded
the advance, and shouted for several hours together,
though not a man could be seen, with the view, of course,
of harassing our small and exhausted force; in which
object they succeeded, for no part has been strong enough

152 THE DEFENCE OF LUCKNOW

to allow of a portion only of the garrison being prepared in the event of a false attack being turned into a real one. All, therefore, had to stand to their arms, and to remain at their posts until the demonstration had ceased; and such attacks were of almost nightly occurrence. The whole of the officers and men have been on duty night and day during the eighty-seven days which the siege had lasted, up to the arrival of Sir J. Outram, G.C.B.

In addition to this incessant military duty, the force has been nightly employed in repairing defences, in moving guns, in burying dead animals, in conveying ammunition and commissariat stores from one place to another, and in other fatigue duties too numerous and too trivial to enumerate here. I feel, however, that any words of mine will fail to convey any adequate idea of what our fatigue and labours have been – labours in which all ranks and all classes, civilians, officers, and soldiers, have all borne an equally noble part. All have together descended into the mine; all have together handled the shovel for the interment of the putrid bullock; and all, accoutred with musket and bayonet, have relieved each other on sentry, without regard to the distinctions of rank, civil or military. Notwithstanding all these hardships, the garrison has made no less than five sorties, in which they spiked two of the enemy's heaviest guns, and blew up several of the houses from which they had kept up the most harassing fire. Owing to the extreme paucity of our numbers, each man was taught to feel that on his own individual efforts alone depended in no small measure the safety of the entire position. This consciousness incited every officer, soldier, and man to defend the post assigned to him with such desperate tenacity, and fight for the lives which Providence had intrusted to his care with such dauntless determination,

APPENDIX IV

153

that the enemy, despite their constant attacks, their heavy mines, their overwhelming numbers, and their incessant fire, could never succeed in gaining one inch of ground within the bounds of this straggling position, which was so feebly fortified, that had they once obtained a footing in any of the outposts, the whole place must inevitably have fallen.

If further proof be wanting of the desperate nature of the struggle which we have, under God's blessing, so long and so successfully waged, I would point to the roofless and ruined houses, to the crumpled walls, to the exploded mines, to the open breaches, to the shattered and disabled guns and defences, and lastly to the long and melancholy list of the brave and devoted officers and men who have fallen. These silent witnesses bear sad and solemn testimony to the way in which this feeble position has been defended. During the early part of these vicissitudes, we were left without any information whatever regarding the posture of affairs outside. An occasional spy did indeed come in with the object of inducing our sepoys and servants to desert; but the intelligence derived from such sources was, of course, entirely untrustworthy. We sent our messengers, daily calling for aid and asking for information, none of whom ever returned until the 26th day of the siege, when a pensioner named Ungud came back with a letter from General Havelock's camp, informing us that they were advancing with a force sufficient to bear down all opposition, and would be with us in five or six days. A messenger was immediately despatched, requesting that on the evening of their arrival on the outskirts of the city, two rockets might be sent up, in order that we might take the necessary measures for assisting them in forcing their way in. The sixth day, however, expired, and they

154 THE DEFENCE OF LUCKNOW

came not; but for many evenings after officers and men watched for the ascension of the expected rockets, with hopes such as make the heart sick. We knew not then, nor did we learn until the 29th of August – or thirty-five days later – that the relieving force, after having fought most nobly to effect our deliverance, had been obliged to fall back for reinforcements, and this was the last communication we received until two days before the arrival of Sir James Outram on Sept. 25th.

Besides heavy visitations of cholera and smallpox, we have also had to contend against a sickness which has almost universally pervaded the garrison. Commencing with a very painful eruption it has merged into a low fever, combined with diarrhœa; and although few or no men have actually died from its effects, it leaves behind a weakness and lassitude which, in the absence of all material sustenance, save coarse beef and still coarser flour, none have been able entirely to get over. The mortality among the women and children, and especially among the latter, from these diseases and from other causes, has been perhaps the most characteristic of the siege. The want of native servants has also been a source of much privation. Owing to the suddenness with which we were besieged, many of these people who might perhaps have otherwise proved faithful to their employers, but who were outside of the defences at the time, were altogether excluded. Very many more deserted, and several families were consequently left without the services of a single domestic. Several ladies have had to tend their children, and even to wash their own clothes, as well as to cook their scanty meals entirely unaided. Combined with the absence of servants, the want of proper accommodation has probably been the cause of much of the disease with which we have been

APPENDIX IV 155

afflicted. I cannot refrain from bringing to the prominent notice of his Lordship in Council the patient endurance and the Christian resignation which have been evinced by the women of this garrison. They have animated us by their example. Many, alas have been made widows and their children fatherless in this cruel struggle. But all such seem resigned to the will of Providence, and many, among whom may be mentioned the honoured names of Birch, of Polehampton, of Barbor, and of Gall, have, after the example of Miss Nightingale, constituted themselves the tender and solicitous nurses of the wounded and dying soldiers in the hospital.

It only remains for me to bring to the favourable notice of his Lordship in Council the names of those officers who have most distinguished themselves, and afforded me the most valuable assistance in these operations. Many of the best and bravest of these now rest from their labours. Among them are Lieutenant-Colonel Case and Captain Radcliffe, whose services have already been narrated. Captain Francis, 13th Native Infantry – who was killed by a round shot – had particularly attracted the attention of Sir H. Lawrence for his conduct while in command of the Muchee Bhawun; Captain Fulton, of the Engineers, who also was struck by a round shot, had, up to the time of his early and lamented death, afforded me the most invaluable aid; he was indeed indefatigable; Major Anderson, the chief Engineer, though, from the commencement of the siege, incapable of physical exertion from the effects of the disease under which he eventually sank, merited my warm acknowledgments for his able counsel. Captain Simons, commandant of artillery, distinguished himself at Chinhut, where he received the two wounds which ended in his death; Lieutenants Shepherd and Arthur, 7th Light Cavalry,

156   THE DEFENCE OF LUCKNOW

who were killed at their posts; Captain Hughes, 57th Native Infantry, who was mortally wounded at the capture of a house which formed one of the enemy's outposts; Captain M'Cabe, of the 32nd Foot, who was killed at the head of his men while leading his fourth sortie, as well as Captain Mansfield, of the same corps, who died of cholera – were all officers who had distinguished themselves highly. Mr. Lucas too, a gentleman volunteer, and Mr. Boyson, of the Uncovenanted Service – who fell when on the look-out at one of the most perilous outposts – had earned themselves reputations for coolness and gallantry.

The officers who commanded outposts – Lieutenant-Colonel Master, 7th Light Cavalry; Major Apthorp, and Captain Sanders, 41st Native Infantry; Captain Boileau, 7th Light Cavalry; Captain Germon, 13th Native Infantry; Lieutenant Aitkin, and Lieutenant Loughnan, of the same corps; Captain Anderson, 25th Native Infantry; Lieutenant Graydon, 44th Native Infantry; Lieutenant Langmore, 71st Native Infantry; and Mr. Schilling, principal of the Martiniere College – have all conducted ably the duties of their onerous position. No further proof of this is necessary than the fact which I have before mentioned, that throughout the whole duration of the siege, the enemy were not only unable to take, but they could not even succeed in gaining, one inch of the posts commanded by these gallant gentlemen. Colonel Master commanded the critical and important post of the brigade mess, on either side of which was an open breach, only flanked by his handful of riflemen and musketeers. Lieutenant Aitkin, with the whole of the 13th Native Infantry, which remained to us with the exception of their Sikhs, commanded the Baillie Guard – perhaps the most important position in the whole of the

APPENDIX IV

157

defences; and Lieutenant Langmore, with the remnant of his regiment (the 71st), held a very exposed position between the Hospital and the Water Gate. This gallant and deserving young soldier and his men were entirely without shelter from the weather, both by night and by day.

My thanks are also due to Lieutenants Anderson, Hutchinson, and Innes, of the Engineers, as well as Lieutenant Tulloch, 58th Native Infantry, and Lieutenant Hay, 48th Native Infantry, who were placed under them to aid in the arduous duties devolving upon that department. Lieutenant Thomas, Madras Artillery, who commanded that arm of the service for some weeks, and Lieutenants Macfarlane and Bonham, rendered me the most effectual assistance. I was, however, deprived of the services of the two latter, who were wounded, Lieutenant Bonham no less than three times, early in the siege. Captain Evans, 17th Bengal Native Infantry, who, owing to the scarcity of artillery officers, was put in charge of some guns, was ever to be found at his post.

Major Lowe, commanding Her Majesty's 32nd Regiment; Captain Bassano, Lieutenants Lawrence, Edmonstoune, Foster, Harmar, Cooke, Clery, Browne, and Charlton, of that corps, have all nobly performed their duty. Every one of these officers, with the exception of Lieutenants Lawrence and Clery, have received one or more wounds of more or less severity. Quartermaster Stribbling, of the same corps, also conducted himself to my satisfaction.

Captain O'Brien, Her Majesty's 84th Foot; Captain Kemble, 41st Native Infantry; Captain Edgell, 53rd Native Infantry; Captain Dinning, Lieutenant Sewell, and Lieutenant Worsley, of the 71st Native Infantry; Lieutenant Warner, 7th Local Corps; Ensign Ward, 48th

158　　　THE DEFENCE OF LUCKNOW

Native Infantry (who, when most of our artillery officers were killed or disabled, worked the mortars with excellent effect); Lieutenant Graham, 11th Native Infantry; Lieutenant Mecham, 4th Oude Locals; and Lieutenant Keir, 41st Native Infantry, have all done good and willing service throughout the siege, and I trust that they will receive the favourable notice of his Lordship in Council.

I beg particularly to call the attention of the Government of India to the untiring industry, the extreme devotion, and the great skill which have been evinced by Surgeon Scott (superintending surgeon), and Assistant-surgeon Boyd, of Her Majesty's 32nd Foot; Assistant-surgeon Bird, of the Artillery; Surgeon Campbell, 7th Light Cavalry; Surgeon Brydon, 7th Native Infantry; Surgeon Ogilvie, sanitary commissioner; Assistant-surgeon Fayrer, civil surgeon; Assistant-surgeon Partridge, 2nd Oude Irregular Cavalry; Assistant-surgeon Greenhow; Assistant-surgeon Darby, and by Mr. Apothecary Thompson, in the discharge of their onerous and most important duties.

Messrs. Thornhill and Capper, of the Civil Service, have been both wounded, and the way in which they, as well as Mr. Martin, the deputy commissioner of Lucknow, conducted themselves, entitles them to a place in this despatch. Captain Carnegie, the special assistant commissioner, whose invaluable service previous to the commencement of the siege I have frequently heard warmly dilated upon, both by Sir H. Lawrence and by Major Banks, and whose exertions will probably be more amply brought to notice by the civil authorities on some future occasion, has conducted the office of provost marshal to my satisfaction. The Reverend Mr. Harris and the Reverend Mr. Polehampton, assistant chaplains,

APPENDIX IV 159

vied with each other in their untiring care and attention to the suffering men. The latter gentleman was wounded in the hospital, and subsequently unhappily died of cholera. Mr. M'Crae, of the Civil Engineers, did excellent service, at the guns, until he was severely wounded. Mr. Cameron, also, a gentleman who had come to Oude to inquire into the resources of the country, acquired the whole mystery of mortar practice, and was of the most signal service until incapacitated by sickness. Mr. Marshall, of the road department, and other members of the Uncovenanted Service, whose names will, on a subsequent occasion, be laid before the Government of India, conducted themselves bravely and steadily. Indeed, the entire body of these gentlemen have borne themselves well, and have evinced great coolness under fire.

I have now only to bring to the notice of the Right Honourable the Governor-General in Council the conduct of the several officers who composed my staff: — Lieutenant James, sub-assistant commissary-general, was severely wounded by a shot through the knee at Chinhut, notwithstanding which he refused to go upon the sick list, and carried on his most trying duties throughout the entire siege. It is not too much to say that the garrison owe their lives to the exertions and firmness of this officer. Before the struggle commenced, he was ever in the saddle, getting in supplies, and his untiring vigilance in their distribution after our difficulties had begun, prevented a waste which otherwise, long before the expiration of the eighty-seven days, might have annihilated the force by the slow process of starvation.

Captain Wilson, 13th Native Infantry, officiating deputy-assistant adjutant-general, was ever to be found where shot was flying thickest; and I am at a loss to

160   THE DEFENCE OF LUCKNOW

decide whether his services were more invaluable owing
to the untiring physical endurance and bravery which he
displayed, or to his ever-ready and pertinent counsel and
advice in moments of difficulty and danger.

Lieutenant Hardinge, an officer whose achievements
and antecedents are well known to the Government of
India, has earned fresh laurels by his conduct throughout the siege. He was officiating as deputy-assistant
quartermaster-general, and also commanded the Sikh
portion of the cavalry of the garrison. In both capacities
his services have been invaluable, especially in the
latter, for it was owing alone to his tact, vigilance, and
bravery, that the Sikh horsemen were induced to
persevere in holding a very unprotected post under a
heavy fire.

Lieutenant Barwell, 71st Native Infantry, the fort
adjutant and officiating major of brigade, has proved
himself to be an efficient officer.

Lieutenant Birch, of the 71st Native Infantry, has
been my aide-de-camp throughout the siege. I firmly
believe there never was a better aide-de-camp. He has
been indefatigable, and ever ready to lead a sortie, or to
convey an order to a threatened outpost under the
heaviest fire. On one of these occasions he received a
slight wound on the head. I beg to bring the services of
this most promising and intelligent young officer to the
favourable consideration of his Lordship in Council.

I am also much indebted to Mr. Cooper, Civil Service,
for the assistance he has on many occasions afforded me
by his judicious advice. I have, moreover, ever found him
most ready and willing in the performance of the military
duties assigned to him, however exposed the post or
arduous the undertaking. He commenced his career in
Her Majesty's service, and consequently had had some

APPENDIX IV 161

previous experience of military matters. If the road to Cawnpore had been made clear by the advent of our troops, it was my intention to have deputed this officer to Calcutta, to detail in person the occurrences which have taken place, for the information of the Government of India. I still hope that when our communications shall be once more unopposed he may he summoned to Calcutta for this purpose.

Lastly, I have the pleasure of bringing the splendid behaviour of the soldiers, viz., the men of Her Majesty's 32nd Foot, the small detachment of Her Majesty's 84th Foot, the European and Native Artillery, the 13th, 48th, and 71st Regiments of Native Infantry, and the Sikhs of the respective corps, to the notice of the Government of India. The losses sustained by Her Majesty's 32nd, which is now barely 300 strong; by Her Majesty's 84th, and by the European Artillery, show at least that they knew how to die in the cause of their countrymen. Their conduct under the fire, the exposure, and the privations which they had to undergo, has been throughout most admirable and praiseworthy.

As another instance of the desperate character of our defence, and the difficulties we have had to contend with, I may mention that the number of our artillerymen was so reduced that on the occasion of an attack, the gunners, aided as they were by men of Her Majesty's 32nd Foot, and by volunteers of all classes, had to run from one battery to another, wherever the fire of the enemy was hottest, there not being nearly enough men to serve half the number of guns at the same time. In short, at last, the number of European gunners was only twenty-four, while we had, including mortars, no less than thirty guns in position.

With respect to the native troops, I am of opinion that

162   THE DEFENCE OF LUCKNOW

their loyalty has never been surpassed. They were indifferently fed and worse housed. They were exposed – especially the 13th Regiment – under the gallant Lieutenant Aitken, to a most galling fire of round shot and musketry, which materially decreased their numbers. They were so near the enemy that conversation could be carried on between them; and every effort, persuasion, promise, and threat was alternately resorted to, in vain, to seduce them from their allegiance to the handful of Europeans, who, in all probability, would have been sacrificed by their desertion. All the troops behaved nobly, and the names of those men of the native force who have particularly distinguished themselves, have been laid before Major-General Sir James Outram, G.C.B., who has promised to promote them. Those of the European force will be transmitted in due course for the orders of His Royal Highness the General Commanding-in-Chief.

In conclusion, I beg leave to express, on the part of myself and the members of this garrison, our deep and grateful sense of the conduct of Major-General Sir J. Outram, G.C.B.; of Brigadier-General Havelock, C.B., and of the troops under those officers who so devotedly came to our relief at so heavy a sacrifice of life. We are also repaid for much suffering and privation by the sympathy which our brave deliverers say our perilous and unfortunate position has excited for us in the hearts of our countrymen throughout the length and breadth of Her Majesty's dominions. – I have, &c.,

(Signed)   T. Inglis,

Colonel, Her Majesty's 32nd, Brigadier

No. V

From the Homeward Mail

A complete nominal list of the officers, members of the Uncovenanted Service, and women and children of the Lucknow garrison; and as the return proceeded from an official source the authenticity may be fully relied on

General Staff

Brigadier-General Sir H. M. Lawrence, chief commissioner, killed; Lieutenant Hutchinson, aide-de-camp; Captain Hayes, military secretary, killed; Captain Edgell, officiating; Captain Wilson, deputy assistant-adjutant-general, contused, recovered; Lieutenant Hardinge, deputy assistant quartermaster-general, twice wounded, recovered; Lieutenant James, sub-assistant commissary general, wounded, doing well; Major Anderson, chief engineer, dead; Major Marriott, pension-paymaster.

Brigade Staff

Brigadier Handscomb, commanding Oude brigade, killed; Brigadier Inglis, commanding the garrison; Lieutenant Birch, aide-de-camp, slightly wounded, recovered; Lieutenant Barwell, town and fort adjutant, officiating major of brigade; Captain Carnegie, provost marshal.

Artillery

Captain Simons, wounded, since dead; First Lieutenant Alexander, wounded, recovered, since killed;

164 THE DEFENCE OF LUCKNOW

First Lieutenant Thomas (Madras); Second Lieutenant Lewin, killed; Lieutenant Brice, wounded, since dead; Second Lieutenant Bonham, wounded three times, doing well; Second Lieutenant J. Alexander, slightly wounded, recovered; Second Lieutenant MacFarlan, wounded, doing well; Second Lieutenant Cunliffe, wounded, since dead.

Engineers
Captain Fulton, garrison engineer, killed; Lieutenant Anderson (Madras) officiating; Lieutenant Innes.

7th Regiment Light Cavalry
Lieutenant-Colonel Master; Captain Staples, killed; Captain Radcliffe, wounded, since dead; Captain Boileau, slightly wounded, recovered; Lieutenant Arthur, killed; Lieutenant Boulton, killed; Lieutenant Warner, adjutant; Lieutenant Martin, killed; Lieutenant Farquhar, wounded, convalescent; Lieutenant Raleigh, killed; Surgeon Campbell; veterinary surgeon Hely, killed; riding master Eldridge, killed.

Her Majesty's 32nd Foot
Lieutenant-Colonel Case, killed; Major Lowe, commanding, twice wounded, doing well; Captain Stevens, killed; Captain Mansfield, dead; Captain Power, wounded, since dead; Captain Bassano, wounded, recovered; Captain M'Cabe, mortally wounded, since dead; Lieutenant Lawrence; Lieutenant Edmonstoune, twice wounded, doing well; Lieutenant Webb, killed; Lieutenant Foster, wounded, recovered; Lieutenant Clery, Lieutenant Brown, Lieutenant Brackenbury, killed; Lieutenant Harmer, wounded, doing well; Lieutenant Cook, slightly wounded, recovered; Ensign

APPENDIX V   165

Charlton, wounded, doing well; Ensign Studdy, killed; Paymaster Giddings; Quartermaster Stribbling; Surgeon Scott, M.D.; Assistant-Surgeon Boyd.

Detachment of Her Majesty's 84th Foot
Lieutenant O'Brien, wounded, recovered; Ensign McGrath.

13th Regiment Native Infantry
Major Bruère, killed; Captain Waterman, wounded, recovered; Captain Germon, Captain Francis, killed; Lieutenant Aitken, Quartermaster, Lieutenant Chambers, adjutant, wounded, doing well; Lieutenant Thain, Lieutenant Loughnan, Ensign Green, dead; Surgeon Pitt.

41st Regiment Native Infantry
Major Apthorp; Captain Kemble, wounded, recovered; Captain Sanders; Lieutenant Ruggles; Lieutenant Graves, dead; Lieutenant Darrah; Lieutenant Inglis, wounded, recovered; Lieutenant Keir; Ensign McGregor, dead; Ensign Hewitt, slightly wounded, recovered; Surgeon Macdonald, dead.

48th Regiment Native Infantry
Lieutenant-Colonel Palmer; Major Bird; Captain Burmester, killed; Captain Green; Lieutenant Huxham, twice wounded, doing well; Lieutenant Smith, Adjutant, wounded (accidentally), doing well; Lieutenant Ouseley, Quarter-master; Lieutenant Fletcher, wounded, doing well; Lieutenant Dashwood, wounded, since dead; Lieutenant Hay, wounded slightly, recovered; Ensign Farquharson, killed; Ensign O'Dowda, slightly wounded, recovered; Ensign Ward; Surgeon Wells, wounded slightly, recovered.

166   THE DEFENCE OF LUCKNOW

71st Regiment Native Infantry

Colonel Halford, dead; Captain Strangways, slightly wounded, recovered; Captain Dinning; Captain Maclean, killed; Lieutenant Langmore, Adjutant; Lieutenant Sewell; Lieutenant Grant, killed; Ensign Worsley, Ensign C. W. Campbell, wounded, doing well; Ensign W. Campbell; Surgeon Brydon, wounded, recovered.

Officers not belonging to the Oude Brigade

Major Banks, Provisional Chief Commissioner, killed; Captain Stuart, 3rd Native Infantry; Lieutenant Fullerton, 44th Native Infantry, dead; Lieutenant Lester, 32nd Native Infantry, killed; Lieutenant Tullock, 58th Native Infantry; Lieutenant Birch, 59th Native Infantry, killed; Ensign Inglis, 63rd Native Infantry, doing duty 13th Native Infantry; Captain Weston, 65th Native Infantry, Oude Frontier Police; Ensign Dashwood, 18th Native Infantry, mortally wounded, since dead.

Oude Irregular Force

Brigadier Gray, Commanding; Captain Barlow, Major of Brigade, wounded, since dead; Captain Forbes, 1st Oude Cavalry, slightly wounded, recovered; Lieutenant Bax, Second in Command, killed; Lieutenant Graham, Officiating Adjutant, dead; Assistant-Surgeon Greenhow; Major Gall, 2nd Oude Cavalry, killed; Lieutenant Shepherd, Second in Command, killed; Lieutenant Barbor, Adjutant, killed; Gentleman Volunteer Fayrer, killed; Assistant-Surgeon Partridge; Lieutenant Graham, Adjutant, 3rd Oude Cavalry, slightly wounded twice, recovered; Lieutenant Clarke, 1st Oude Infantry; Captain Hughes, 4th Oude Infantry, wounded, since dead; Lieutenant Soppitt, 4th Oude Infantry; Assistant-Surgeon Hadow; Captain Hawes, 6th

APPENDIX V   167

Oude Infantry, wounded, recovered; Lieutenant Grant, Second in Command, wounded, since dead; Apothecary Thompson; Lieutenant Graydon, 7th Oude Infantry, very dangerously wounded, since dead; Lieutenant Watson, Second in Command; Lieutenant Mechamns, Adjutant; Lieutenant Vanrenen, 9th Oude Infantry; Assistant-Surgeon Darby, M.D., 10th Oude Infantry; Captain Hearsey, unattached; Captain Orr, unattached.

Assistant Chaplains of Lucknow
The Reverend H. P. Harris; the Reverend H. S. Polehampton, wounded, since dead.

Civil Surgeons
Surgeon Ogilvie, Superintendent of Jails; Assistant-Surgeon Fayrer, Residency Surgeon.

Gentlemen of the Civil Service
Mr. Gubbins, Financial Commissioner; Mr. Ommanney, Judicial Commissioner, killed; Mr. Cooper, Secretary, Chief Commissioner; Mr. Martin, Deputy-Commissioner, Lucknow; Mr. Benson, Deputy-Commissioner, Durriabad; Mr. Capper, Deputy-Commissioner, Mullaon; Mr. Lawrence, Officiating Deputy-Commissioner, Gondah, wounded, recovered; Mr. Thornhill, Assistant-Commissioner, Lucknow, slightly wounded, recovered – dangerously wounded, since dead; Mr. Boulderson, Assistant-Commissioner, Lucknow, slightly wounded, recovered.

Ladies and Children in Garrison
Mrs. Hayes and child, Mr. Edgell and child, Mrs. Marriot, Mrs. Inglis and three children, Mrs. Barwell and child, Mrs. Thomas and child (Mrs. Thomas, dead),

168 THE DEFENCE OF LUCKNOW

Mrs. Lewin and two children, Mrs. Staples, Mrs. Radcliffe and three children (one child dead), Mrs. Boileau and three children, Mrs. Case and sister, Mrs. Steeven, Mrs. Giddings, Mrs. Bruère and four children, Mrs. Germon, Mrs. Aitken, Mrs. Pitt and child, Mrs. Apthorp and child (child dead), Mrs. Darrah and two children, Miss Palmer killed, Mrs. Bird and two children (one child dead), Mrs. Green (dead), Mrs. Huxham and two children (one child dead). Mrs. Ouseley and three children (two children dead), Mrs. Dashwood and three children (one child dead), Mrs. Wells and child, Mrs. Halford, Miss Halford, Mrs. Strangways and four children (one child dead), Mrs. Brydon and two children, Mrs. Stuart and child, Mrs. Banks and child, Mrs. Birch, Mrs. Orr and child, Mrs. Hearsey, Mrs. Barlow, Mrs. Forbes and three children (two children dead), Mrs. Graham and two children (one child dead), Mrs. Gall, Mrs. Barbor, Mrs. Clarke, Mrs. Soppitt, Mrs. Grant and child (both dead), Mrs. Watson and child, Mrs. Harris, Mrs. Polehampton, Mrs. Ogilvie, Mrs. Fayrer and child, Mrs. Gubbins, Miss Nepean, Mrs. Ommaney, two Misses Ommaney, Mrs. Couper and three children, Mrs. Martin and two children (two children dead), Mrs. Benson and child (child dead), Mrs. Thornhill and child (child dead), Mrs. Schilling, Mrs. Hale and child, (both dead), Mrs. Fullerton and child (child dead), Mrs. Dorin, killed; Mrs Kendall and child (child dead), Mrs. Bartrum and child (child dead), Mrs. Clarke and child (both dead), Mrs. Anderson and child (both dead), Mrs. Anderson, Dr. Mrs. Boileau and four children (one child dead), Miss E. E. Birch.

European Women and Children in Garrison
Mrs. Evans, dead; Mrs. Brett and child (child dead),

APPENDIX V 169

Mrs. Ball and child; Mrs. Cane and three children; Mrs. Court and two children; Mrs. Connell and child; Mrs. Grant; Mrs. Abbott and child (child dead); Mrs. Hembro and three children; Mrs. Purcell and child; Mrs. Longton and child; Mrs. Morgan; Mrs. Sexton; Mrs. Ramsay; Mrs. Watson and child; Mrs. Ryder; Mrs. Wells and child; Mrs. Woods and three children (one child dead); Mrs. Morton and child (child dead); Mrs. Baxter and three children; Mrs. Fitzgerald and child; Mrs. Fitzgerald and three children (one child dead); Mrs. Martin; Mrs. Kinsley and four children; Mrs. Rae; Mrs. Gabriell and three children; Mrs. Pew, senior; Mrs. Pew, junior, and four children (two children dead); Mrs. Ireland and child; Mrs. Swarris and three children; Mrs. Gambooa; Mrs. Blyth and child (child dead); Mrs. Jones; Mrs. Luxted; Miss Luxted; Mrs. Catania; Mrs. Forbes; Mrs. Blaney; Mrs. Hyde and two children; Mrs. Sequera, senior; Mrs. Sequera, junior, killed; Mrs. Chrestien; Miss Sequera; Mrs. Vaughan and two children; Mrs. Beale; Mrs. Hardingham; Mrs. Sinclair; Miss Hampton; Mrs. Elliott; Mrs. Sangster and two children; Mrs. Barnett and child; Miss Sangster; Mrs. Browne; Mrs. Hamilton and three children (two children dead); Mrs. Velozo; Miss Velozo; Mrs. Horn and three children; Mrs. Parry and four children; Mrs. Ereth; Mrs. Bates; Mrs. Scott and child (child dead); Mrs. Need and three children; Mrs. Higgins, dead; Mrs. Williams and child (child dead); Mrs. Wilkinson, dead; Mrs. Allnutt and child (child dead); Mrs. Reilly and child (child dead); Mrs. Collins and child (both dead); Mrs. Macgrenan; Mrs. Garland and child; Miss Clarke; Mrs. J. J. Phillips; Mrs. W. Phillips and child; Mrs. Leslie; Mrs. Lincoln and child; Mrs. Chick and two children (one child dead); Mrs. Clancey and two children; Mrs. Joyce and child; Mrs. Best and child (child

170   THE DEFENCE OF LUCKNOW

dead); Mrs. Pidgeon; Mrs. Todd and child; Mrs. Blunt; Mrs. Garrett and two children; Mrs. Pedron; Miss Marshall; Miss Savaille; Miss Campagnac; Mrs. Dudman and three children (two children dead); Mrs. Ward and child; Mrs. Dudman 2nd; Mrs. Rennick; Mrs. Derozario; Mrs. Dacosta; Mrs. Archer and two children; Mrs. Hilton and two children; Mrs. Dera Vara and two children; Mrs. Pender and four children; Mrs. McDonnough and two children; Mrs. Oliver and two children; Mrs. Brown; Mrs. Rontleff and child; Mrs. Curwan and child; Mrs. Lynch and child; Mrs. Moreton and two children (both children dead); Mrs. Smith and three children; Mrs. Brandoff; Mrs. Curtain and three children; Mrs. Kennedy; Mrs. Bally and two children; Mrs. Peter; Miss Kennedy; Mrs. Burnet and child; Mrs. Cook and four children (one child dead); Mrs. Bryson and four children (one child dead); Mrs. Marshall; Mrs. Rutledge and two children; Mrs. Lawrence and two children (one child dead); Mrs. Samson; Mrs. Horan and three children; Mrs. Kavanagh and four children (one child dead); Mrs. F. Marshall and two children; Mrs. Sago; Mrs. Virtue; Miss Virtue; Miss Brown; Mrs. F. Williams and two children; Mrs. Gordon and two children; Mrs. Hoff; Mrs. Wittenbaker and eight children; Mrs. Donnithorne and two children (one child dead); Mrs. Pearce and two children; Mrs. Mendes, dead; Miss Gardner; Miss Roberts; Mrs. Dubois, senior; Mrs. Dubois, junior; Mrs. Campagnac, senior; Mrs. Campagnac, junior, and four children; Miss Campagnac, 1st; Miss Campagnac, 2nd; Mrs. Mahar and two children; Mrs. Twitchem; Mrs. Marley and one child; Miss Hampton; Mrs. Longden; Miss Rodgers; Mrs. Duff and child; Mrs. Griffiths and three children; Mrs. Keogh and five children (three children dead); Mrs. Molloy and five

APPENDIX V 171

children; Mrs. Hernon and four children; Mrs. Bickers and three children; Mrs. Barrett and three children (one child dead); Mrs. Casey and five children (one child dead); Mrs. Alone, Miss Alone; Miss Arno; Miss Robinson; Miss Bowhear; Mrs. Johannes and child; Mrs. Queiros and child; Mrs. Dias; Mrs. Pelling; Mrs. Nazareth and two children (Mrs. Nazareth, dead); Mrs. Nugent, junior, and three children; Mrs. Joseph and three children; Mrs. Hamilton; Mrs. Blenman; Mrs. Bates and child; Mrs. Barfoot.

Members of the Uncovenanted Service

Messrs. J. F. Macgrenan, R. Garland, W. E. Fitzgerald, R. M. Collins, F. Leach, F. Williams, F. Knight, J. Gordon, E. Hoff, R. Dorrett, Anthony Wharton, Wittenbaker, Wittenbaker, junior (killed), S. Williams, Donnithorne, Velozo, Pearce, Mendes (killed), Phillips, French, Leslie, Lincoln, Chick, W. Phillips, Clancey (killed), Ewart, Todd, R. Joyce, Thriepland Blund, Forrester (wounded), Potter, Kavanagh, Marshall, Forder, May, Martin, Morgan (wounded), McRae (wounded), Bryson (killed), J. Brown (killed), C. Brown (killed), O. Browne (dead), W. Marshall (killed), E. Sequera (killed), Blancey (wounded, recovered), Rutledge (wounded, recovered), Duhan, Hutton, Owen, Morgan, Lawrence, Sarle, Sequera, Parey, Allnutt, B. Alone, A. Alone (wounded), A. Bates, Blenham (wounded), Bailey (wounded, recovered), Bickers (wounded), Ereth (killed), T. Catania, C. Catania, Hardingham, Rees, J. Sinclair (wounded), McAuliffe (killed), Sinclair (pensioner), Rae, Gabriel, Samuels, Pew, sen., A. Pew, jun., G. Ireland, W. Ireland, Swarries (wounded, recovered), Fernandes, Blythe, Jones, Luxted (pensioner), Hyde (wounded, slightly recovered), Howard, Forbes, Blaney, Deprat (killed), W.

172 THE DEFENCE OF LUCKNOW

Hamilton, Sequera, Sequera, jun. (wounded, recovered), Chrestien, Schmidth (wounded, since dead), Collins, Vaughan (wounded, recovered) Elliott, Sangster, Beale (killed), Queiros, Queiros, junior, Queiros 3rd, Johannes, Nazareth, Dias, Signor Barsotelli, Jeoffry, W. Brown, Mitchell, Johnson, Symes, Wells (killed), Dubois, Campagnac, C. Campagnac, B. Dudman, Owen, Hill, Crabb (killed), Need (killed), Ward, Barry, Casey (dead), Barrett (dead), Wiltshire (dead), Macmanus (killed), Cameron (dead), Gerald Cameron (merchant), H. H. Birch (son of the late Lieut.-Col. F. W. Birch).

Martiniere School
   Mr. Schilling, Principal; Mr. Crank, Assistant; Messrs. Archer, Dodd, Wall, Hilton, Dera Vara, De Verrine, and boys.

THE END